WHAT DO YOU SEEK?
Monastic Wisdom for Living Today

What Do You Seek?

Monastic Wisdom for Living Today

John-Francis Friendship

CANTERBURY
PRESS

Norwich

This book is dedicated to all
Anglican Religious Orders
that we might learn from their wisdom.

A M D G

© John-Francis Friendship 2021

Published in 2021 by Canterbury Press
Editorial office
3rd Floor, Invicta House,
108–114 Golden Lane,
London EC1Y OTG, UK
www.canterburypress.co.uk

Canterbury Press is an imprint of Hymns Ancient & Modern Ltd
(a registered charity)

Hymns Ancient & Modern® is a registered trademark of
Hymns Ancient & Modern Ltd
13A Hellesdon Park Road, Norwich,
Norfolk NR6 5DR, UK

British Library Cataloguing in Publication data

A catalogue record for this book is available
from the British Library

978-1-78622-345-6

Typeset by Regent Typesetting
Printed and bound by
CPI Group (UK) Ltd

Contents

Foreword

BY THE BISHOP OF MANCHESTER

Ferrets were entirely unknown to Peruvian Anglicans. I was due to make a long stay and was advised to take photos of my home life to share at various gatherings and had taken shots of my wife, children and pets. The cats they instantly recognized but, even using the correct Spanish word, a ferret meant nothing to them.

For many, the Religious Life is as unknown as my ferrets. We might know 'monk' and 'nun' but nothing of what enlivens those words. Yet, Archbishop Welby has repeatedly said, there can be no revival of Christianity without the renewal of the Religious Life. His colleague in York, Stephen Cottrell, adds a historical context reminding us that Europe was not evangelized by clergy, but by monastics.

During the time I have chaired the committee bringing together representatives of Church of England Religious Communities alongside our bishops, I've closely witnessed how a fresh burst of the Holy Spirit has drawn Christians to exploring and engaging with new forms of the Life and its traditional expressions. Emerging communities are learning from experienced brothers and sisters as they explore how patterns of living out baptismal life can be strengthened by the wisdom passed down through many centuries of Religious Life. I vividly recall one leader of an emerging community, not from the Catholic end of Anglicanism, telling me, 'We've discovered St Benedict – it's all there, isn't it?' Her words left me wondering how many more sense being drawn to something, but with no better idea of what it might be than my Peruvian friends did of my ferrets, and so fail to find their true calling.

This book is written for those wanting to grow in their discipleship, as the title indicates; those who may not have the language or pictures adequate to describe, even to themselves, the nature of that precious pearl for which they are searching. It concerns Anglican Religious Life and comes bearing the experience of one deeply formed as a Franciscan but who has spent many years drinking at the wells of a variety of expressions of the Life. Key features are set out simply and clearly, illustrated from the writings of many who have travelled this way before; reinforced by both Scripture and the words of the Desert Elders.

Perhaps this book should be required reading for all presenting themselves to their Vocations Team or priest, who feel God's call must, because this is the only model they have ever seen, mean becoming a 'vicar'. In our pluriform age, consideration of Religious Life should be required of those who seek to help people find their path among today's array of options.

Above all this is a book for *any* prepared to acknowledge that what they are seeking is not merely to better themselves, who acknowledge that the small voice from within will be quietened neither by enthusiastic activity nor internal contemplation, but by recognizing that this call comes from beyond. The one we are seeking is God, and we seek because God has already sought us. The Holy Trinity summons us to a closer fellowship, lived out in that communal companionship which encompasses both activist and hermit. It is God who calls us to a life that can only be lived in God's grace and God's strength.

+ *David Manchester*
(Chair of the Advisory Council for Religious Communities)
Christmas, 2020

Acknowledgements

I am deeply grateful to all who assisted in my vocational development as I sought to respond to God's call on a journey that continues to be rich, varied and adventurous and which has informed this writing. In setting out to explore aspects of my subject I'm thankful to those communities who helped my research: the Benedictine nuns of St Mary's Abbey, Malling (whose singing is one of the hidden gems of this treasury), the monks and nuns of Mucknall Abbey, the Community of the Holy Name, the Community of St Mary the Virgin, the Community of the Servants of the Will of God, the Sisters of the Love of God and the Society of the Precious Blood, all of whom gave hospitality. It was a privilege to be invited into the privacy of their Enclosures and meet with members who gave their time and shared their wisdom. Their sense of dedication was matched by humour and humility as we explored the treasures their Life offers to the Church. I was assisted in visiting them by a grant from the Clergy Support Trust. Thankfully, I was able to visit before the 2020 pandemic struck bringing a halt to further expeditions.

I also want to thank the All Saints Sisters of the Poor, the Community of the Resurrection, the Community of the Sacred Cross, the Community of the Sisters of the Church and the Society of St John the Evangelist whose help was greatly valued. Other Orders kindly provided written information and Pusey House, Oxford allowed me access to archival documents. His Eminence Archbishop Angaelos of the Coptic Church in the United Kingdom graciously shared his wisdom and gifts.

Paul Alexander TSSF and John Heath acted as 'critical friends' as did Sr Clare-Louise SLG, Fr Colin CSWG, Fr James

Koester SSJE, Br Nicholas Alan SSF, Br Stuart OSB (Mucknall Abbey) and Br Tobias n/SSF who – amid full lives – read, commented on and corrected my writings. As ever, the editorial staff at Canterbury Press were helpful.

Thanks also to Abigail Lily CHF, Aileen CSC, Anita Woodwell SGS, Bernard OC, David Clayton, Mary John OSB, Mary Joy SSB, Fr Nicholas Buxton, Sarah Jane Clarke, Fr Louis Darrant and Stephen Hogg for their help and Dr Peta Dunstan for checking details concerning historical accuracy.

Finally, I want to thank Chris, my partner, without whose continuing support and encouragement this book could not have been written.

Glossary

ANCHORITE: the name applied to someone who has made a vow to remain in their hermitage, often attached to a church.

ANGLO-CATHOLIC: that understanding of Anglicanism that recognizes its continuity with the pre-Reformation Church. In the early nineteenth century, the Oxford Movement, starting in the University, restored much that had been lost in terms of ecclesiology, theology and spirituality, including the Religious Life. Many priests and Religious moved into the growing slum parishes because they believed Christ was to be especially found and served there. They also opened up traditions of Orthodox spirituality.

ASCETIC/ASCETICISM: concerns forms of self-denial that help develop a life in Christ.

BLESSED SACRAMENT: the consecrated bread and wine of the Eucharist, the outward and visible form of Christ's Body and Blood.

CHARISM: gifts of the Holy Spirit that informed the founder of an Order and continues to give it life for the benefit of the Church and the world.

CHOIR: the place in a Chapel where Religious pray together.

COMPUNCTION: a momentary sorrow, regret, or sense of remorse at having done, or contemplated doing, something wrong.

CONTEMPLATION: taking time to gaze with the eye of the heart at something in depth – a 'long, loving look at the real' (Walter Burghardt SJ).

CONTEMPLATIVE LIFE: enables contemplation, often through Religious vows. 'Active contemplatives' is a term applied to those who, living in the world, seek to do so contemplatively.

CONTEMPLATIVE PRAYER: the silent gaze of the soul upon God who returns that gaze, leading to repenting of whatever separates us and increasing our desire to live with deepening love. It comes either as an unmerited gift or is gifted through prayer.

DAILY/ DIVINE OFFICE (known as the Liturgy of the Hours): psalms, scripture readings and prayers forming the official prayer of the Church. It includes Vigil Matins (very early in the morning), Lauds (Morning Prayer), Terce, Sext (Midday Prayer), None, Vespers (Evening Prayer) and Compline (Night Prayer).

DISPERSED COMMUNITIES: Religious living under vows but not in community, although normally meeting at agreed intervals.

DEVILS, DEMONS, SATAN: terms used to refer to those forces that lead us away from the light of Christ. Today we might also speak of inner movements or external forces.

ENCLOSED: Religious living the monastic/contemplative life who are focused into the place (enclosure) where they live. Such separation may involve boundaries defined by walls and grilles with entry only permitted to lay people (i.e., not Religious) for specific purposes. The purpose of enclosure is to prevent distraction from the life and to protect the prayerful silence of the place. Those living in such enclosure may only leave it by permission.

EREMITICAL LIFE: that form of life adopted by HERMITS – women and men living in seclusion out of devotion to God. Terms such as SOLITARIES, ANCHORITES or RECLUSE are also used.

EUCHARIST/MASS/HOLY COMMUNION: the name given to that service in which Christ's sacrifice is remembered in the context of the supper he shared with his disciples on the night before his crucifixion. That meal has been understood as the Passover meal (Exodus 12) which Jews celebrate to bring into the present their liberation from slavery in Egypt. Through preparation we are nourished by this sacrament of his Body and Blood.

GRACE: God's gift working on human nature for our good.

KINGDOM/REIGN OF GOD: that which concerns godly living/society which we pray for in the Our Father (Lord's Prayer).

LITURGY (*work of the people*): a public act of worship.

METANOIA: a fundamental, transformative change of heart.

MONASTIC: living through the vows of stability, conversion of life and obedience. The word is also used to describe those living those vows (a 'monastic').

NOVITIATE: length of time spent as a novice.

OFFICE: see DAILY/ DIVINE OFFICE

OTHER: a way of referring to God.

RELIGIOUS: the term is used in either a collective sense to describe a particular way of life under vows or to describe individuals who follow that life (Sr = Sister/Br = Brother/Fr = Father/Mthr = Mother). 'Religious' was the term Fr Benson SSJE used as shown by his early writings and talks.

SACRAMENTS: Baptism and the Eucharist, together with Confession, Confirmation, Anointing of the Sick, Ordination and Marriage, are outward and visible signs conveying God's grace.

SACRAMENTALS: other recognized means (e.g., holy water) carrying a blessing.

SCAPULAR: a long piece of cloth placed over the shoulders. There are two kinds: one worn by Religious and the other being devotional to remind the wearer of the spirituality of an Order.

SOUL: the immortal aspect of our being created by God.

SPIRITUAL DIRECTOR: someone, lay or ordained, who is gifted with the ability to attend to another as they seek to understand and respond to God's call.

Introduction

When you search for me, you will find me;
if you seek me with all your heart.
(Jeremiah 29.13)

This is a book about a life that has nurtured the Church for almost 2,000 years yet is hidden from the view of many. Present in the Anglican Communion for almost two centuries, it is known by few even though it focuses the essence of faith. At a time when some believe the way to renew the Church and make it appealing is through adapting aspects of popular Western culture, there's still a hunger and thirst for that spiritual food which Religious have offered for centuries.

As I write this, I'm listening to a recording of ancient and modern plainchant by Poor Clares that topped the charts for weeks. The Church may be wondering how to touch people, but these enclosed sisters have immediately connected with non-believers through plainsong written for just that purpose – to open us to the Divine – yet often ignored by the Church. Religious Life is custodian of a treasury of freely available wisdom, and my primary purpose is to show what it can teach us about the essence of life in Christ. I've also had in mind those considering their call: too often 'vocation' is limited to 'ministry' yet from the time Anglican Orders reappeared in the early nineteenth century until the turn of that century more than 10,000 women alone responded to the call (Mumm 1999, p. 209). Most were fired by the Oxford Movement which, beginning in 1833, enabled the Church – often in the face of violent opposition – to recall its catholic roots severed at the Reformation, not least those which aid sanctification.

Christian community comes in many forms and what follows isn't intended to be a history of Religious Life nor an introduction to every Anglican Order, although stories will be told. And because the Life concerns more than just 'monks and nuns', I use the traditional term 'Religious' to describe anyone living under vows. If other words are unfamiliar there is a Glossary, while more basic information can be found in my book *The Mystery of Faith: Exploring Christian Belief* which I wrote for those concerned to understand more about the Faith. Appendix 1 also gives some details of the Orders mentioned, each being identified by initials (e.g., CR, Community of the Resurrection) which also appear after names, showing the Order to which a Religious belongs. Traditionally this indicated the name of the new 'family' into which they had entered (e.g., Brother *N*, CR).

What's the purpose?

Many feel overwhelmed by the brokenness of our world and some want to 'do' something to address its problems. Religious share that sense but know they need, first, to be rooted in God; that anything they 'do' must be the consequence of that ever-deepening relationship.

Some think Religious lock themselves away, but most aren't 'enclosed', not least the Franciscans whose founder, St Francis of Assisi (1182–1226), considered the world his cloister. I joined them in 1976 and, looking back, am amazed at the enriching diversity of what I did, who I met and where I travelled – and how challenged I was. This led one of the pioneers of Anglican Religious Life, Fr Richard Meux Benson SSJE (1824–1915), to argue that it's not a job or being a particular kind of person but a calling by God to God; a Life that is one of the great means of spiritual instruction for the Church – an outward and visible sign of what the Church is called to be. Through their consecration, Religious are yeast, reminders that we're all called to be hidden with Christ in God (Col. 3.3f.); people who 'tend a fire that cannot go out', in the words of an anonymous Carthusian.

It's a Life evoking that of the first Christians:

All who believed were together and had all things in common; they would sell their possessions and goods and distribute the proceeds to all, as any had need. Day by day, as they spent much time together in the temple, they broke bread at home and ate their food with glad and generous hearts, praising God and having the goodwill of all the people. (Acts 2.44–47)

Such a witness had profound eloquence because, aided by humility, love and joy, it revealed the appeal of lives centred on the mystery of God, something that's meant to apply to every church community.

We ... seek to live in an atmosphere of praise and prayer. We aim to be constantly aware of God's presence, so that we may indeed pray without ceasing. Our ever-deepening devotion to the indwelling Christ is a source of strength and joy. It is Christ's love that inspires us to service and strengthens us for sacrifice. (Third Order of the Society of St Francis, *The Principles of Life*, Day 14)

The Way of Love

The object of the Society of Saint Francis
is to build a community of those who accept
Christ as their Lord and Master,
and are dedicated to him in body and spirit.
They surrender their lives to him,
and to the service of his people.
(SSF, *Principles*, The Object)

According to the Church of England website, Religious Life is a form of consecrated life within the Church: 'Recognised

Communities are those which are organised along the traditional (monastic) vows of stability, conversion of life and
obedience, or what are known as the 'evangelical counsels' of
poverty, chastity and obedience' (www.churchofengland.org./
life-events/vocations/religiouslife).

Although that radical (idealized?) witness described in Acts
2 proved unsustainable the call continued. To be a Christian is
to reflect the way we discover our identity when realizing ourselves as part of the body of Christ. We are nourished by him
and the Eucharist is central to that body, a public affirmation
that through sharing one bread and one cup, we affirm that
divisions are to be overcome as, together, we seek to live his
sacrificial life.

> Every Christian is called to live in community as a member
> of the Church. Christ in his wisdom draws each disciple into
> that particular expression of community which will be the
> best means of his or her conversion. (SSJE, *Rule*)

People have been attracted to the Religious Life as it witnesses
to the ordering of the great commandments: '… you shall love
the Lord your God with all your heart, and with all your soul,
and with all your mind, and with all your strength' and 'You
shall love your neighbour as yourself' (Mark 12.30–31). Made
in the image of the triune God, we're to discover our identity
primarily through relationship.

A consecrated life

We also need this Life because it witnesses to our baptismal
consecration and without Religious the Church may forget
important aspects of that consecration. Rather than a social
construct, it is the sacramental expression of the mystery of
God, and behind whatever ministry an Order has its members
– first and foremost – are given to God as they say, with Mary:
'let it be with me according to your word' (Luke 1.38).

We do not come into our Community principally to convert others, but rather with the desire, first of all, to be converted ourselves. Then, if by God's grace we are converted to Him, He must use us in missionary work, or in any other way that He pleases ... (Benson SSJE 1911, p. vi)

Many sense that there's 'more' to life and, while they can't describe exactly what that is, feel there's almost another person they could be – so this book tries to explore ways in which this Life addresses that feeling. How there's a 'hidden monk' in everyone.

On becoming a Christian, I realized that if God existed there could be nothing of greater importance upon which to set my heart. Trying to grow in Christ I visited various communities and was deeply impressed by the way each expressed something of what it means to follow him. My first encounter was with the Community of St Mary the Virgin at Wantage when I was 16 and that visit was profoundly moving. Their worship, aided by plainsong, one of the great treasures promoted for general use through the Catholic Revival, had a depth previously unknown. I was familiar with Anglican chant, which even our church choir struggled with at times, but the simple way the sisters sang enabled a prayerfulness, reminding me of that saying attributed to St Augustine: 'The one who sings (well), prays twice.'

Later I stayed with the Benedictines at Nashdom Abbey, visited the Society of St John the Evangelist and, while engaged in the usual teenage activities, felt attracted to this Life. Something stirred within me (cf. John 6.25ff.) and, when I encountered Franciscans, sensed I 'belonged'. Just as Abram heard a call and stepped out in faith (Gen. 12) I needed to respond to the way God seemed to be calling (cf. Gen. 17.5) and discovered the truth of what Augustine *did* say: 'O God, you have made us for yourself, and our hearts are restless until they rest in you' (*Confessions* I, 1).

Follow me

Like others, my teenage years were confusing, but Christ was knocking on my heart asking to inhabit the whole of me; his request was loving and peaceful and something awoke as I responded. For a long time I'd wanted to *do* something for God and was considering ordination, but here was a field containing treasure for which I was prepared to sell everything (Matt. 13.44):

> Listen! I am standing at the door, knocking;
> if you hear my voice and open the door,
> I will come in to you and eat with you, and you with me.
> (Rev. 3.20)

After joining the Franciscans my vocation blossomed as brothers (and sisters) inspired, encouraged, enlivened (challenged, annoyed and irritated) me. They accepted me when I fell and were intent on the one thing that mattered – to follow Christ in the way of little Poor Man of Assisi.

> [Religious Life] is an attempt to live the gospel life and suffer the consequence. If we are trying to live really by love and not by the Law – that is in risk, exposure, and constant impingement upon each other – then it will indeed be only by the grace of God that we can stay 'nailed to the cross of our Order'. (Jane SLG 1994, p. 16)

What Franciscans and others show is something of the simplicity and joy, struggle and beauty of life abandoned to God. We may not be asked, as Jesus asked one young man (Matt. 19.21), to sell our possessions but when, at the end of the Eucharist, 'we offer (God) our souls and bodies to be a living sacrifice' we need to risk meaning that and go into the world with a heart filled with thankfulness and an awareness of divine glory in all things.

Religious Life is the witness of life surrendered in death, surrendered in death that God may transform it into life. (Fr Gilbert Shaw, Warden of the Sisters of the Love of God, 1962–67, unpublished talk)

A Rich Variety

'I am the way, and the truth, and the life.'
(John 14.6)

Christ's call has challenged many, and the two main forms of Religious Life – 'monastic', bounded by the cloister, and 'active' (or 'apostolic', those sent out) – can seem contradictory. To confuse matters more, the term 'monk' (or 'nun') and 'monastic' is often applied to all, yet since the time of St Francis of Assisi different forms of Religious Life have developed which is why this book concerns all forms and not just monasticism.

Monks, nuns and others

Though both St Benedict (c. 480–543) and St Francis sought places of solitude (and Francis allowed some brothers to lead a more solitary life) the search for God can never be a 'flight of the alone to the Alone' (Plotinus, c. 205–c. 270, *Enneads*, VI, 9, ix), *nor* simply a means of social transformation. Embracing Christ's cross which, rooted in the earth and rising to heaven, has arms enfolding the world, these forms are complementary. Many Anglican founders attempted to bring them together in a 'mixed life', placing as much emphasis on the Eucharist, Daily Office, and times of silence and solitude as on practical service.

Our community exists, not that we may be bound to one-another, but that we may be the better individually bound to Christ. (Benson SSJE 2020, p. 159)

While the works undertaken by some were obvious – nursing, teaching, ministerial formation, evangelism – the charism that animated their founders was usually hidden. So, we will look at what inspired them and reflect how the Church, increasingly caught up in management, can learn from their age-old wisdom.

Today, when some are attracted by living as 'active contemplatives', communities that blend monastic living with evangelical outreach have considerable insight to impart. Most welcome guests and many provide opportunities for people to share in their life as Alongsiders, while others offer Internships, Schools of Life and so on. In their wisdom all witness to the importance of the slow work of God who strips us to remake us as we follow the way of the cross. Prayer needs to be our heartbeat and worship our lifeblood and, intentionally, we need to give ourselves to God and ask how we might serve. But you don't have to enter a community to live this way – many do so in the context of their own homes as external oblates, Tertiaries, Associates or Companions.

If we really love God, everything will be freely and gladly given, regardless of what we feel in terms of consolations or awareness of him.
(Jane SLG 1994, p. 20)

'New monasticism'

Often referred to as 'New Religious Communities', this diverse movement – which can be Christian or non-Christian – involves commitment to a simple Rule including elements of common life. Back in the early 1970s, I belonged to a small residential community at the church of All Saints in London's West End, where one of the first Anglican Orders had been founded. We made no vows, had our own jobs, but shared aspects of community life including daily worship, study programmes and meals. Although aided by two Religious sisters, whose wisdom helped us as we sought to travel the way of Christ, we never considered ourselves to be 'monks' or 'nuns'.

Later I took part in attempts to establish Base Ecclesial Communities (Basic/Small Christian Communities) in the UK. These lay-led initiatives, originating in poorer regions of Central and South America, attempt to return the Church to its original calling. Embedded in their neighbourhoods they listen to what Jesus' good news is saying while seeking to be agents of change for a more just society. This has had a profound effect in many parts of the world, not least in Africa where Archbishop Emeritus Desmond Tutu, a Franciscan Tertiary, realizing the movement as an expression of *ubuntu* – that catholic notion of humanity, 'I am because we are' – has been a leading supporter.

Seeking wisdom

Religious Life needs directing and moulding by the wisdom of Jesus, Word of the Father, whom we're to desire, seek and incarnate through our lives. We may have taken this Life too lightly and need to wake up to the treasures it contains in earthen vessels. It may not sparkle with the same allure as some aspects of the Church but is its most precious gift and prophetic witness. Thankfully, some still realize this and know that the spirituality that flows through it can refresh us at times when the Church can feel a little lost, a little shallow – a little in need of the 'wisdom of the ages'.

At heart, it's a way of expressing those baptismal promises to die to sin, renounce evil and reject the devil. Its wisdom is of value to all who want to respond to God's call, who recognize the need for that *metanoia* – change of heart – which alone brings peace and joy as we turn, again and again, to Christ, our Saviour and Lord.

Religious Life is a function of witness and labour,
the total commitment of self,
holding nothing back
in order to be the channel of God to the world.
(Fr Gilbert Shaw, unpublished talk to the Sisters of the
Love of God)

For the Love of God

'Unless a grain of wheat falls into the earth and dies,
it remains just a single grain; but if it dies, it bears much fruit.
Those who love their life lose it,
and those who hate their life in this world
will keep it for eternal life.
Whoever serves me must follow me,
and where I am, there will my servant be also.'
(John 12.24–26)

It was Maundy Thursday 1976 and the Mass of the Last
Supper had begun when I arrived at Hilfield Friary, home to a
large community of brothers of the Society of St Francis (SSF).
Set on the northern slopes of the Dorset Downs, I'd driven the
final few miles through lanes studded with primroses and cow-
slips before turning off into what had been a farmyard. Along
one side lay the chapel created from an old cow-barn where,
on entering, I felt a need to 'kneel where prayer has been valid',
as T. S. Eliot wrote in *Little Gidding*.

Surrounded by the Divine in nature and liturgy, this Life
seemed to offer something of immense importance. It was as
if I'd arrived at the start of something; the questing I'd experienced and the way I'd felt increasingly out of step with the
world suddenly didn't trouble me. I sensed being invited into
a deeper relationship with Jesus, to love and serve him in the
way of St Francis who, joyfully, beckoned me to follow. The
struggle to have any priestly vocation recognized fell away:
the doorway through which I'd passed into the mystery of the
Eucharist opened to my future.

I needed (and still need) to give attention to what I encoun-

tered: a community living out the Parable of the Loving
Father (Luke 15.11–32) where, knowing myself a sinner, I felt
welcomed. What was the point of seeking to make ever-more
money, having the latest car, promoting myself (and being
judged), becoming a 'success' when none of that really satisfied? Here was an invitation to step out of the rat-race and
stand in the presence of God who called into my emptiness.
The Life touched the deepest place of my being, offering a
glimpse of a 'new Eden' where I could start afresh with Christ,
the new Adam, who spoke once to another youth: 'If you wish
to be perfect, go, sell your possessions, and give the money to
the poor, and you will have treasure in heaven; then come,
follow me' (Matt. 19.21).

After we had left the altar having fed on Mystic Food,
I discovered that the community opened its doors for other
'wayfarers' who had tramped the lanes to this place of hospitality. I reflected on sharing supper with Brothers, guests and
those who found it difficult to fit into society, realizing this *was*
a taste of kingdom living where all things were being created
anew. Here was hospitality human and divine – the essence of
Religious Life – accepting us, warts and all. Much later, when I
became Guest Brother, I discovered that many valued the way
they knew the brothers wouldn't judge them by those 'warts'
but were there to share their burdens.

Called by God

The Lord called Samuel again, a third time.
And he got up and went to Eli, and said,
'Here I am, for you called me.'
Then Eli perceived that the Lord was calling the boy.
Therefore, Eli said to Samuel,
'Go, lie down; and if he calls you, you shall say,
"Speak, Lord, for your servant is listening."'
(1 Samuel 3.8–9)

When Eliot wrote about 'kneeling in prayer' he was recalling the chapel in Little Gidding, Huntingdonshire where, during the reign of Charles I, its manor house became home to an attempt by Nicholas Ferrar, scholar, courtier and deacon, to develop a community involving his extended family. It lasted from 1626 until 1657 after which, for much of the following century, the Church of England lapsed into a stupor before two revivals began – first Evangelical and then Catholic. But Ferrar's community was considered 'romish' and the foundations that had sustained the Church for one and a half millennia were mostly swept away until, on 26 March 1845, Jane Ellacombe, a young woman who became known as Sr Anne and died nine years later, began living a form of solitary Religious Life near London's Regent's Park.

> Catholic Christianity is for all, for the whole of man, and for all time. The church cannot be national, nor exclusive, it is for all. It is only in the Church that real equality is to be found – where all are baptised with one baptism and all partake of one bread. (Raynes CR 1959, p. 57)

Letting go of my old life didn't prove easy, and I resisted the process at times, especially as aspects of my 'self' needing redemption were revealed. That's what happens if, like the Mother of Jesus (she-who-listened), we say 'yes' to God – even tentatively. As time went on, I realized this (often painful) remaking and reshaping was the most important thing that can happen – more important, and more satisfying, than any external makeover – if we are to reflect God's glory. That is what makes us fully human, and it begins with turning the eye of the heart to God with faith, hope and love.

> We must remember that our life as Religious is not some-thing over and above the ordinary Christian life. It is only the ordinary Christian life developed under such regulations as are rendered necessary for individuals, because the Church at large has fallen away from her true spiritual calling of conscious and habitual union with Christ. (Benson SSJE 1900, p. 6)

Beginnings and Endings

'If any want to become my followers, let them deny
themselves and take up their cross and follow me.
For those who want to save their life will lose it,
and those who lose their life for my sake will find it.
For what will it profit them if they gain the whole world
but forfeit their life?'
(Matthew 16.24–26)

Giving up home, job and friends wasn't easy but, beneath my
fears, I felt the drawing of Love, for these endings were the
means of a new beginning. Slowly, I began to discover that
deeper than the attraction of other loves lies the call of One
who longs to draw us into union, a union we read existed 'in
the beginning'. Before any talk of sin and the 'Fall' there's the
account of how humankind bears the image of its Creator who
was pleased – delighted – with creation (Gen. 1.31) and lived
in harmony with all things.

The wonder of creation

Now I live in a city I often walk in our nearby ancient woodlands. Depending on the season I can breathe the aroma of dead
leaves, feel the sharpness of frost, see the greenness of foliage,
and sense a deep, intimate at-oneness. I can open myself to
the Creator by looking with my inner eye beneath those outer
forms into creation's heart. As I do, I realize a sense of wonder
which enables thankfulness, a thankfulness leading to deep joy.

Genesis tells of how we became a living human being when
God breathed into our flesh, a primal act about which the
hymn at Night Prayer (Compline) reminds us:

O Father, that we ask be done
Through Jesus Christ, your only Son;
And Holy Spirit, by whose breath
Our souls are raised to life from death.

Religious Life is an attempt, by the grace of God, to nurture fertile ground from which God might bring about a new creation. It invites us to open our 'nostrils' to God's inbreathing; to regain the divine image by giving primary attention to loving God. Such a life might be 'on the edge' but its focus is reconciliation; just as God is a Trinity of Persons existing in a never-ending communion of love, so Religious Life invites us to make real Christ's prayer, 'thy kingdom come'.

Existential crisis

That invitation can speak powerfully if, lost in the speed and demands of life, you want quality rather than quantity. Gradually – suddenly – I saw beyond what money buys, tasted a freshness of faith, and awoke to the need to live at one with all.

> The earth is filled with the Spirit of God,
> Creative, powerful, free,
> Encounter as wind unseen.
>
> Sweep through our hearts and renew us in God,
> Life-giving breath from high,
> Love's energy working love.
>
> Sing to his glory, fling wide his praise,
> People redeemed and set free,
> Caught in the shout of heaven's joy.
> (OSB Malling, Office hymn: Terce)

Having forgotten our calling and grasped at the fruits of creation, we need to learn that the way to paradise is by the hard road of repentance, something those Elders, the Fathers (Abbas) and Mothers (Ammas) of the Middle Eastern deserts, knew to be fundamental, as we will discover.

Recall for a moment that incident concerning our primal forebears: 'They heard the sound of the Lord God walking in the garden at the time of the evening breeze, and the man and his wife hid themselves from the presence of the Lord God among the trees of the garden. But the Lord God called to the man, and said to him, "Where are you?"' (Gen. 3.8–9). Where are you? Having gone my own way, felt in control and could do as I liked, I began to know myself as part of the whole. Now I realize that, if humankind is to survive, we need to regain a profound respect for creation in all its divine beauty, repent of our folly and understand that we must not hide from our responsibility towards a world brought into being by an outpouring of love.

Called into being

Looking back, I realize that much of my life has concerned a struggle to be found and nurtured by love. There was a time when I wasn't sure I'd been loved, and confused love with casual sex. It's not that I've never *been* loved but needed to allow my heart-restlessness to centre into a deepening desire for union with the Sacred, divine Heart, which is why Paul's words are so profound:

> I pray that, according to the riches of [God's] glory,
> he may grant that you may be strengthened
> in your inner being with power through his Spirit,
> and that Christ may dwell in your hearts through faith,
> as you are being rooted and grounded in love.
> I pray that you may have the power to comprehend,
> with all the saints, what is the breadth and length
> and height and depth, and to know the love of Christ
> that surpasses knowledge,
> so that you may be filled with all the fullness of God.
> (Eph. 3.16–19)

The desire to know the boundless riches of Christ (Eph. 3.8) has drawn many into Religious Life and invigorated all they did. At best, their ministry expressed his love flowing through them, an example of the truth of Jesus' words to the woman at the well: 'The water that I will give will become … a spring of water gushing up to eternal life' (John 4.14). Having drunk that living water, they longed for others to taste it.

But no life is plain sailing and community life isn't perfect; made up of ordinary people there were times I found some brothers hard to live with. I never knew what it was like to be angry until I joined community! At other times life could be grey, or I felt depressed or struggled to love an offending brother. It's easy to fall foul of the lure of perfectionism and scrupulosity and forget that Christianity embraces life's paradoxes. There were days I felt lost and, wistfully, looked back to what I had left behind – which usually causes problems (cf. Gen. 19.26). You can sense that dilemma in the story of the young man who asks Jesus how to find eternal life but can't let go of his possessions, causing him desolation (Luke 18.23). Then, in chapter 19, there's an account of the freedom and fullness that came to Zacchaeus as he, freely and generously, responded to Christ's call.

Each time I read Mark's account of Jesus' encounter with the rich man (10.17–22) I'm struck by the way Jesus looked on him with love and often sense that a culture that constantly tempts us with superficialities will distract us from the gaze of God's compassionate face. Yet it's by lovingly returning that gaze we come to fullness of life; we need to pray to be formed by Love into what Love longs for us to become. What both Church and world need are people seeking to love God, and Religious Life is a reminder that this is the primary call for all Christians.

Yet when I listen to some talking about vocation it's often about *doing* things for God even though, as the pioneers of Religious Life knew, 'doing' must be rooted in prayer. That's why those involved in encouraging people to ponder their calling need to urge them to consider Religious Life with its invitation to be 'sacraments' of Christ. An invitation that can be disconcerting, but which simply requires our 'yes' to what God desires, a 'yes' which will affect the whole cosmic order, as we'll see.

Seeking Home

When you search for me, you will find me;
if you seek me with all your heart,
I will let you find me, says the Lord,
and I will restore your fortunes
and gather you from all the nations
and all the places where I have driven you, says the Lord,
and I will bring you back to the place
from which I sent you into exile.
(Jeremiah 29.13–14)

'What do you seek?' That question posed by Jesus (John 1.38) can, if we listen, help us consider our fundamental desires. While realizing the need for necessities, Religious Life enables attention to be given to what was said by anyone at their Franciscan novicing: 'I seek God and his will for me.'

This desire, lying at the heart of faith, is often referred to in the Scriptures: 'Seek the Lord and his strength, seek his presence continually' (1 Chron. 16.11); 'You speak in my heart and say, "Seek my face." "Your face, Lord, will I seek"' (Ps. 27.11). To 'seek God's face' speaks into a longing for at-oneness; it's easy to let other things – no matter how important – get in the way, but this invitation needs to be held in the heart of all Christ's servants.

Desiring at-oneness

I know I can only become fully human when my desire is to be united with the Divine. It's a journey leading through times of fear and failure, falling and becoming besmirched by life's messiness. I didn't find it easy to respond to the call to serve others, abandon my will and die to self, yet, in spite of times of darkness, there have been moments of light and hints of new life till, one day, I will come to face my Judge and Saviour.

O Christ you lover of mankind,
shine your never waning light on our hearts
who sing to you in faith,
granting us the peace of God which passes all understanding;
so that by fleeing from the darkness of sin
to the light of your righteousness,
we may glorify you;
for you are the One God
with the Father, and the Holy Spirit,
now and for ever and ever. Amen.
(CSWG, Troparion before the Invitatory,
Office of Vigils, Wednesday Week 2)

Humility

'He must increase, but I must decrease.'
(John 3.30)

Priscilla Lydia Sellon, born in 1821 into a wealthy upper middle-class family, shocked many when she gave up her comfortable life to go and live in a Plymouth slum where she developed a school for 'wild and neglected children' and set about trying to live as a nun. That was in 1848 when she was just 27 and within two years Mother Lydia, as she became known, had established 20 different social projects, founded the first stable Anglican Religious Order (the Devonport Sisters, later the Society of the Most Holy Trinity) and is now acknowledged as 'Restorer of Religious Life in the Church of England'.

Given her background what she undertook involved a profound letting go of the past and the acceptance of the way of humility, not least because of the abuse and aggression she faced. What she did went against every Victorian norm and many were angry that this 'protestant' was embracing 'catholic practices'. But, at heart, she was only doing what Christ had done; for his loving, humble obedience brought him to live among us even to death and, through that act, opened for us the gates of paradise.

Lord, I am not worthy

This matter of humility, fundamental to (Religious) life, mustn't be confused with self-loathing. Rather, the beauty of the soul is unmasked through accepting ourselves as we really are (in the sight of our compassionate God). False coverings of self-pride are stripped away and, nurtured by compunction – the 'prick of sorrow' – we experience contrition for our failings. It isn't a fashionable virtue yet spoke into the heart of Mother Lydia and others: 'Not my will but yours.' Their example invites me to look to Christ and, keeping my gaze on him, ask the question, 'how does he see me?' And then saying: 'Jesus, I trust you'.

Trust can be difficult but is the root of healthy humility. As a Benedictine nun of Malling said to me: 'By the expansion of one's awareness of the presence of God we can be weaned from our innate self-centredness; from what *I'm doing* to an awakening of what God may be doing, bringing to birth, in me. We are being reborn into our true, native soil of *humus*, humility.'

> Do not think too much of yourself. Your own opinions and feelings may well be of less importance than they seem to you.
> (SSM, *Principle XXII*)

But some have been deeply hurt and are inclined to self-defensiveness. Fear of the 'other' can run deep and we need to value ourselves and acknowledge our achievements and abilities while recognizing the corrosive effects of pride, leading St Bernard of Clairvaux to observe:

No spiritual house can stand for a moment
save on the foundation of humility.
(SSF, *Principles*)

Each month I listened to readings from those Principles which
informed our life and realized how little I manage(d) to practise the virtue of humility: '... brothers and sisters must also
refrain from all contemptuous thoughts one of another, and
not seeking for pre-eminence must regard others as better than
themselves. The faults that they see in others must be subjects
for prayer rather than criticism and they must be more diligent
to take the log out of their own eye than the speck out of their
neighbour's eye.'

How self-centred I am! How slow to relish the goodness and
giftedness of others! I've craved affirmation, sought approval
and experienced deep shame when, eventually, I've come to
my senses (cf. Luke 15.11f.). I've wanted to be right rather
than owning my faults (in the confessional); dwelling on them
has been seductive and prevented that thankfulness that comes
from realizing God wants to welcome me: 'No, I'm not perfect – here's just another example – what more do I expect of
myself! But, by God's mercy, I will be forgiven and restored
when I return to him. And then I need to forget myself.' We all
fall yet Christ is there (though we may not know it) encouraging us, with deep compassion, along the way – and if we do get
things wrong, he'll let us know.

O Lord I am not proud: I have no haughty looks:
I still my soul and make it quiet,
like a child upon its mother's breast:
my soul is quieted within me.
(Ps. 131.1, 3)

Seeing myself through Christ's merciful eyes requires me to
look to him; look at the figure of the crucified and know that
he died because of his love – for *me*.

To see ourselves in the mirror of God is the beginning of penitence, and penitence is the foundation of spiritual life and growth. We can go no distance along the road to heaven unless we are penitent.

(Raynes CR 1959, p. 95)

My prayer needs to be shaped by looking to the One whose humility can raise me up; whose praises, if I sing them, can open my heart and set it free. The One who showed that greatness comes through being the servant of all, not by lording it over them.

Know thyself

I was fortunate to once attend a church where a life-sized crucifix greeted those who entered. There, before my eyes, was displayed the humility of God who doesn't condemn; there Love looked down and I needed to offer myself to him. Later, when I learned that the basis of any spiritual life is 'know thyself', I understood I was invited to do so in the gaze of someone who knows the cost of being real. Of being humble. That was among the first lessons I learned as I was encouraged to own both my failings *and* giftedness, while seeking the lowest place rather than praise and esteem (but giving that to others).

We learn the humility of self-loss, which is the heart and secret of the contemplative way, as we wait for all the unconscious tensions in ourselves to come up that we may offer them in penitence to God, waiting also in complete dependence on him when the pressures from the world outside close in upon us. (Fr Gilbert Shaw, Homily for Sunday after the Ascension, 1966)

Slowly I discovered I couldn't hide from my brothers and gained much as I became exposed to their (sometimes painful) gaze that saw through my masks, while all the time being held in Love. That is what makes community such an important means of growth; I had to accept myself as flawed but loved, able yet self-centred and then give thanks *for* that self. Instead of seeing everything through the distorting lens of pride, I began to know that our worth isn't dependent on anything but Love.

> I could feel myself opening to God's presence. Of course, this lack of distraction also confronts us with ourselves, with no opportunity to run away. This growing in self-knowledge is an important part of the Benedictine journey. (Malling Abbey nun)

Yet, as Sr Benedicta Ward SLG wrote, 'God does not impose goodness on anyone, but what he waits for is the humility that can trust what is outside the limiting circle of the self' (Ward SLG, *The Way Supplement*, 1989, p. 17).

> What God is waiting for is not a right conclusion about a matter but for our suppleness in falling into his hands for him to work in us.
> (Ward SLG, *The Way Supplement*, 1989, p. 14)

Accepting brokenness

Slowly I realized how often I projected my 'stuff' on to others or scapegoated them for my own sinfulness. Like someone who pushes their dirty washing into a cupboard, shuts the door and then lets it fester, I'd promote my virtues and insist on being right at all costs. Yet only by acceptance of imperfections and seeking the helpful grace of God can the path towards wholeness be trod: 'Why do you see the speck in your neighbour's eye ...' (Matt. 7.3). Humility lightens the path to repentance; repentance to confession, and confession to healing.

It's a hard way. I don't always want to be compassionate, generous to those in need, live with thanksgiving – own my sin – and one of the hardest things was living with brothers who opened that cupboard door revealing the things I'd stuffed there. Yet what they offered was precious as, slowly, I learned to accept myself – the way of Mary's *Magnificat*:

... he has looked with favour on his lowly servant ...
and has scattered the proud in their conceit,
casting down the mighty from their thrones
and lifting up the lowly.

Clothed with humility

I've been privileged to know many who lived with real humility, showing that 'God opposes the proud, but gives grace to the humble' (1 Peter 5.5f.). People who, like Br Damian SSF, don't fear lowliness, knowing God chose to be born of a mother who wanted to be a servant; Mary who, penetrated by the Spirit, knew the ease with which we can acquiesce to the troublings of our disordered desires.

Recognizing these movements, we can delight in the compunction they cause in a heart set on God – who loves a humble heart (Phil. 2). Like Christ's (Matt. 11.29) ours must become lowly as we open it to the Spirit who wishes to rule there.

We desire to be as empty vessels, empty of all pride, self-righteousness, love of place and power, so that we may be fulfilled with God's grace. And because praise tends to quicken pride, and calumny to humble us, we would learn to rejoice when men speak ill of us, and to be afraid when we are praised. (Br Douglas SSF from Seaver and Coleman 1960, p. 26)

In a talk to his community, Fr Colin CSWG once said: '... humility comes from a profound understanding of the mercy of God, shown to us by sending his only Son to save us. The monk's humility comes from seeing himself as the one on whom God has shed his mercy and so he treats others as the same as himself. They are also ones on whom God has shed his mercy, so the monk must be merciful too.' Perhaps this prayerful exercise might help:

23

- Imagine Jesus as a baby in the crib and ask – why does he lie there? What brought him among us?
- Consider his life and listen to his teaching – how does that speak into your heart?
- Look at his suffering – how does that move you? What do you want to say to him?
- Place yourself before a crucifix. Imagine Christ gazing on you and ask: what does he long for, for me?
- Silently allow every feeling to be present and, at some point, express those feelings by word or write them in a spiritual journal. Ask Jesus how he wants to change you.
- Then, asking for the help of the Holy Spirit, pray for grace to help your will support your desire: 'thy will be done on earth as it is in heaven'.

Offering Self – the Way of Holiness

As the eyes of servants look at the hand of their masters,
and the eyes of a maid to the hand of her mistress,
so our eyes look to the Lord our God,
until he show us his mercy.
(Psalm 123.2)

In the end, Religious Life is meant to be a way of holiness, of wholeheartedly responding to the One who calls. Having summoned creation into being, God called Abraham, Moses, the Prophets – and in Christ the call to *new* life became explicit. God, of course, calls everyone: we mustn't forget that we owe our life to God and that, for life to be fulfilled, it must be surrendered to and directed by God. Made in the image of One who delights in being reflected in us, we will only be complete when we return to love's source and let it flow through us. So, at times I pray:

Jesus Christ, love of God,
have mercy on my sinful heart.

Just as a child gains identity through the family and nation into which it is born and the Christian through baptism into the body of Christ, so the Religious gains their identity by 'birth' into their community. I vividly recall feeling that 'new birth' when clothed in the brown Franciscan habit and wanting this 'new man' to grow. Deeply conscious of entering a stream that had flowed for centuries, I longed to abandon myself to that movement. Gradually I understood that our basic nature isn't changed in a moment but, cooperating with the Holy Spirit, grace can slowly work *on* nature to bring about a new creation.

The primary purpose of Religious Life is to offer a way which leads to eternal life and to enable that life to permeate this life. A Religious is called to withdraw so that the Holy Spirit of God might flow through the space brought about by the way they are seeking to create a new heart by repentance. Their simple dependence on God – their obedience – brings healing to the disease of humankind's conflicting interests and their desire to dominate the world – and their neighbour – through the power of their ego. (Fr Gilbert Shaw at the Commissioning of Bede House, Kent, 20 August 1966)

Jesus said the fulfilment some seek, which can be an expression of self-preoccupation, was the way to becoming lost (Luke 17.33); if you really want to find *life* you need to let go of the search and be prepared to be lost and desire to be found in him. It's a long struggle as we are purified and strengthened by fighting all those 'demons' – those impulses and drives – that tempt us away.

The Christian stands in a place of conflict ... it is not an easy place to stand. It is not easy because we feel the pressures of the world telling us to give up or to give into pleasing the self ... The steadiness of prayer and of offering is what is required, and God will do with it as he sees fit. (Fr Colin CSWG, Pre-Pentecost Community Retreat, 2017)

The Beatitudes

As the Catholic Revival developed it became clear that the theology and spirituality it was rediscovering affected social questions. As some became wealthier, a few 'fashionable women' began to feel uncomfortable with their life of self-gratification which wasn't providing the happiness it promised. They felt challenged by what they read in their Bibles and heard Jesus' teachings about the road to blessedness (Matt. 5.3f.; Luke 6.20f.). In their desire to grow they heeded the same call that led Francis to leave the wealth of his family and dwell among lepers, and so went to do the same among the poor. Blessedness concerns the way we live.

If we truly think of Christ as our source of holiness, we shall refrain from anything wicked or impure in thought or act and thus show ourselves to be worthy bearers of his name. For the quality of holiness is shown not by what we say but by what we do in life. (St Gregory of Nyssa, from a treatise on *Christian Perfection*)

Mary and Martha

But lest we consider the essence of Christianity is about 'doing good', the account of Mary and Martha offers a startling surprise (Luke 10.38–42). When I began life at Hilfield one of the first lessons I learned was that everything had to stop when the bell for chapel rang – it's so easy to let 'doing' rule our life. But when Jesus was asked about the most important commandment, he didn't immediately say 'serve your neighbour', he quoted the Shema (Deut. 6.4, 5) recited by Jews twice each day: 'Love the Lord your God with all your heart, and with all your soul, and with all your mind' and, consequentially, your neighbour – as yourself (Lev. 19.18). So, when hard-working Martha complained that her sister was doing nothing but sit at Jesus' feet, rather than reprimanding Mary, he commended her, reminding Martha that sitting in contemplative wonder was a good thing.

Such an observation can be hard to hear – why *did* Jesus say that? Why *does* love of God come before love of neighbour? Religious Life, with its emphasis on prayer, profoundly challenges the Church to consider its call. Are we informed by the desire that people be drawn to the vision of God or by the norms of our activist world?

Christian life concerns this call to holiness, to the revelation of God shining in the world, and that's where we need to keep centred. Clergy, in particular, need to remember that beneath their role is this call to be rooted in the intimate dance of the soul with its Maker; beneath all the good things we do there needs to be this desire for God, something that becomes almost *tangible* in some. Most of us can be attracted by people who seem to have something we would like – success, ability, fame, looks, money and so on, but saintly lives have a richer, deeper appeal. An appeal that can be challenging, and that challenges *me* to consider on what my own heart is set.

Love calls to my heart's core
and, bending my ear,
a warmth seeps from that silent place
of encounter.

2

Seeking God

The Call of the Desert

He sustained him in a desert land,
in a howling wilderness waste;
he shielded him, cared for him,
guarded him as the apple of his eye.
(Deuteronomy 32.10)

For six weeks during my novitiate I lived at Shepherd's Law, a hermitage built in the remoteness of the Cheviot Hills of Northumberland in the latter part of the twentieth century by Br Harold SSF. I had gone there to experience something of the solitary way, and with caravans for eating, sleeping and prayer and one tap for (cold) water, it was a formative time. What I came to realize is that while such a life might seem lonely, the hermit's solitude can become the place of communion.

> For the solitary, his solitude is the *milieu* for his growth in a mature relationship with God and the knowledge of God's will for the world. For him withdrawal emphasises the fact of his relationship with man, because through the deepening of his prayer in solitude he comes to a deeper realisation of his co-inherence in mankind. (Shaw 1979, p. 7)

Anyone living alone or drawn to the solitary life realizes it's not an easy way. It involves facing loneliness and oneself while denying the ego-driven self and overcoming that babble of tempting, taunting and damaging voices which the Desert Elders called 'evil spirits'.

> Regardless of whether we believe in the reality of spiritual beings (demons), maybe today we would call them neurosis or complexes, it is true that in this struggle with thoughts such as jealousy, anger or despair, we are up against fearsome opponents. (Br Nicholas Alan SSF, correspondence with the author)

The desert is present everywhere. Sometimes we are driven there, or we might choose to enter it – or ignore it. However, if we do, we will never discover the inner, sacred cave in whose deep, dark recess is the stream of life. The place of waiting, of simply being-there as we encounter our true self and God together with those 'wild beasts' (Matt. 1.13) with whom we'll need to wrestle. Yet whether in remote places or city suburbs, whoever has dwelt there can offer a wealth of vital insights into human life and flourishing.

Purity of heart

Hearing Jesus say that it is those whose hearts are pure who will see God (Matt. 5.8), many entered the desert seeking to cooperate with the Spirit in that work of cleansing the heart. This is the Opus Dei to which all Christians are called (Ward SLG and Russell 1979, p. 26). One of the Desert Elders, John Cassian (AD 360–c. 435), wrote in his *Conferences* (1.4, 5–6) that while the goal of the spiritual life is the 'vision of God', its more immediate focus is 'purity of heart'. Solitude helps us discover what lies there and consider what, by grace, needs changing to regain the divine image through *metanoia*, conversion of the heart. So it is that the Jesus Prayer has become important for many monastics: 'Lord Jesus Christ, Son of the living God; have mercy on me, a sinner'. 'The substance of the Jesus prayer,' wrote Br Ramon SSF, 'is both a petition to the divine compassion and an adoration of the divine love'

(Ramon 1989, p. 119). It's a petition arising from a deepening sense of our own sinfulness, a sense that is not intended to be overwhelming but to keep us attentive to the loving mercy of God and awaken us to pray: 'Create in me a clean heart, O God; and renew a right spirit within me' (Ps. 51.10).

But this need to cleanse the heart doesn't only concern individuals – there are dark forces at work in the world. Many entered the desert because they saw it as the source of those demons (Isa. 34.14; Matt 12.43) who sought to obscure the Light and undermine humankind, and wanted to fight them with the weapons of faith and prayer. It's the particular call of hermits to engage in this struggle and the Church mustn't forget that the world needs them, and pray that God will move people to consider this call.

Repentance

From the Elders to the Third Order of St Francis of Assisi, whom he named 'Penitents', Religious Life concerns repentance and the primary responsibility of the Church is to proclaim that need for a change of heart, which one sister described as 'moving out of one's centre and letting God move in'.

Penitence can act as a deterrent to pointing the finger, so when we need to confront corruption it must be with a humble heart knowing that we are also sinners. Repentance keeps us conscious of our need of mercy and is part of the way we grow in him who seeks to wean us of self-concern, freeing us to love with purity of heart: stripped of our old-self that a new-self, the Christ-centred self, might emerge.

> To see ourselves in the mirror of God is the beginning of penitence, and penitence is the foundation of spiritual life and growth. We can go no distance along the road to heaven unless we are penitent. (Raynes CR 1959, p. 95)

The Desert

O God, you are my God; eagerly I seek you,
my soul thirsts for you, my flesh faints for you,
as in a barren and dry land where there is no water.
(Psalm 63.1)

Just off the desert road between Cairo and Alexandria lies Wadi Natroun, an area home to hundreds of monks. Their monasteries, mostly founded in the early Christian era, have experienced a remarkable renaissance over the past 50 years as engineers, professors and doctors fill the cells and people flock to these 'oases of the Spirit' to pray or take the sick for healing. I once spent a retreat at one of them, St Macarius, and apart from being plagued by flies, was deeply grateful for the hospitality and holiness of that community.

Ever since our ancestors began to consider themselves in relation to the wider world, we've experienced that sense of incompleteness which can only be answered as the heart's depths are touched by that for which we were made – union with the 'Other'.

From the time we lived as hunter-gatherers there's evidence humans sensed being part of a spirit-filled world (see, for example, Wright 2010). Even when people say they don't believe in God, many are aware of a desire for a 'spiritual experience'. Fr Gilbert Shaw would remind the Sisters of the Love of God of the distinction between the Christian way and this search for a 'spiritual' way: the latter involves an 'experience' but the former concerns a surrender to the Lover who wants to re-make us.

The Elders, realizing that the divine image within us needed restoration, knew that could only be done through the conversion of their heart – through trusting in the faith they professed. Their life consisted of prayer, especially reciting the psalms, and simple manual labour as they sought to say, with St Paul: 'it is no longer I who live, but it is Christ who lives in me' (Gal. 2.20). This required the 'old man' in them to die so that the life they lived in the flesh could be lived by faith in the Son of God, 'who loved me and gave himself for me' (Gal. 2.19f.).

The Greening of the Desert

Lord, you have searched me out and known me;
you know my sitting down and my rising up;
you discern my thoughts from afar.
(Psalm 139.1–2)

Over 3,000 years ago, deep in that Fertile Crescent sweeping through modern-day Iraq, a man heard a call to leave his home city of Ur and travel into the vast wilderness stretching westwards. Abram (which means 'Exalted Father') set out and, faithful to that call, eventually settled in a distant country, later becoming known to Jews, Christians and Muslims as 'Abraham' ('Father of a Multitude'), the father of three faiths.

Later, after encountering God in a burning bush (Ex. 3), Moses led the Israelites for 40 years in their exodus through another wilderness and, on a mountain peak, made a covenant with God on behalf of the people (Ex. 19f.) before they entered God's 'promised land'.

Elijah fled into the desert where, at the entrance to a mountain cave, he heard a 'sound of sheer silence: the presence of God' (1 Kings 19). His life has since inspired countless hermits, pointing to the importance of the 'cave of the heart', the inner cell we need to inhabit – the 'womb' of the soul.

John the Baptist, Jesus' cousin, possibly spent time with the Essenes, that radical Jewish movement with communities in the desert. Afterwards he appeared in the wilderness calling people to repent, a call that continues to be made to those seeking to follow Christ of whom John said: 'He must increase, but I must decrease' (John 3.30).

Jesus also recognized the importance of the desert and, apart from spending forty days in one where he was tempted by the devil (Matt. 4), often retreated to such places for prayer.

By the third century, thousands had begun living as hermits in the deserts of Egypt, Palestine, Syria and parts of Turkey. They recognized the importance of Jesus' words: 'whenever you pray, go into your room and shut the door and pray to your Father who is in secret; and your Father who sees in secret will reward you' (Matt. 6.6), and so sought out solitary places where they lived in cells. Some did so to avoid persecution but after that ceased and the Church became increasingly powerful, others wanted to separate themselves from the obvious temptations presented by this development. They desired a place where dependence rests on God alone, or did so in imitation of Christ or to fight the fallen angels/evil spirits dwelling there (Isa. 34.14; Matt. 12.43), forces that drove the demagogues of their age who, often using religion, were corrupting many. Today, Religious are only allowed to embark on the solitary way once it's clear this call is from God and not a means of escaping communal life, and anyone believing they have a similar calling needs to be accompanied by a wise spiritual director who understands the vocation.

Shared solitude

Pachomius (d. 346), an ex-soldier, developed a Rule by which solitaries might come together, but it's St Anthony of Egypt (251–356) who is called the 'Father of All Monks'. Having heard Christ's call to give his possessions to the poor he spent many years living alone before writing a simple Rule for those who began gathering around him. In seeking to develop their alternative communes they recalled Jesus' words: 'As the Father has loved me, so I have loved you; abide in my love. If you keep my commandments, you will abide in my love, just as I have kept my Father's commandments and abide in his love' (John 15.9–10).

Anthony's monastery in the Eastern Desert is still filled with monks and popular with pilgrims, but he eventually retreated to a cave for the rest of his life. There he sought at-one-ness with him who is the beginning, the firstborn from the dead, in whom all the fullness of God was pleased to dwell (Col. 1.18–19).

Monks to earth's ends

The Life quickly spread along the trading routes of the Roman Empire and attracted many to places on the edge, be that hot, arid places or windswept islands such as Lindisfarne, Bardsey, Iona – hermitages on the Celtic fringes. The inner eye of the solitary stretches as far as it can, challenging us to look beneath the horizons of our world.

> It is possible to be a solitary in one's mind
> while living in a crowd,
> and it is possible for one who is a solitary
> to live in the crowd of his own thoughts.
> (Amma Syncletica, fourth-century Desert Elder)

Turning from the ways our culture can appeal to the baser aspects of our humanity involves more than simply avoiding sin; it requires us to 'cultivate stillness and practice contemplation' (Ward SLG and Russell 1979, p. 32) and nurture humility. We discover at-oneness with creation by renouncing our disordered desires – that selfishness that can entrap the heart – cultivating the 'virtues' and overcoming the 'vices' so that our true Christ-likeness might be revealed.

Virtues and vices

The path to purity of heart is guided by the Virtues, a way rarely spoken of today. But as Religious communities developed, they realized that holiness involves cultivating:

Prudence
Justice
Temperance
Fortitude
Faith
Hope
Charity

The dangers of their opposite Vices were also recognized along with their remedies:

Pride (Humility)
Envy (Kindness/Gratitude)
Anger (Meekness/Self-control)
Laziness (Diligence)
Greed (Generosity)
Gluttony (Temperance)
Lust (Chastity)
(Felix Just SJ, catholic-resources.org)

In an unpublished sermon preached to the Sisters of the Love of God in 1964, Fr Gilbert Shaw reminded them that the practice of self-discipline isn't for the sake of staying out of trouble or the avoidance of a guilty conscience, but in order that we might acquire those virtues, 'not by our own effort (the Pelagian heresy prevalent today) but by cooperation with grace'.

In the emptiness of the desert/wilderness the dark forces we struggle with become more apparent. The Elders talked about 'spiritual warfare' between light and darkness (Eph. 6.10f.) as, with God's help, they faced a battle within their hearts (Rom. 7.21f.).

For my enslavement to the passions I deserve condemnation, therefore I turn to you, O blessed Forerunner of the Lord, and earnestly beg your help, for you were chosen above all others, and you now shine out before Christ our joy. Look down, O Herald of repentance, upon my afflicted heart and see the wounds of my soul and help forward my salvation by your holy prayers in the presence of the Lord our God. Amen. (CSWG, Troparion at Vespers, Week 1, Ordinary Time)

Apatheia

Knowing that cultivating a Christ-like heart would involve a fight to renounce those primitive drives ('passions') which, if out of control, lead into sinful action (Titus 3.3) the Elders sought to let the Spirit take charge and drew on the ancient practice of *apatheia*. Unlike the English word 'apathy', this concerns developing a profound inner calm which detaches a person from overwhelming passions by cultivating their opposites within the context of Godly love.

This teaching is important today when we are encouraged to express our feelings and social media is awash with rage. Is my response guided by the 'foolish' teachings of Christ and his saints or by the 'wisdom of the world' (1 Cor.1.21f.)? The 'demon' of anger delights in deceiving us, causing Evagrius Ponticus (AD 344–395) to say: 'When you are tempted, do not fall immediately to prayer. First utter some angry words *against the [demon]* who afflicts you' (The Praktikos 42). In this way we are released from passion's grip by turning the tables on the tempter.

Fasting

They fasted to strengthen their resolve to be filled by God through having more time for prayer. Fasting usually concerned food and many of the first Anglican Religious, who would have previously enjoyed a lavish lifestyle, practised this discipline – sometimes excessively.

In *The Religious Vocation*, Fr Benson noted that as we have lost the power of fasting the missionary work of the Church had 'deteriorated'. The Church 'has sought rather to feast upon the good things of the world than die to the world that it may know the blessed feast of Paradise and may win that feast by exercising the strength of God' (p. 214f.). Although any practice of fasting should be discussed with a spiritual director it can help us resist the things of the 'world', and hunger for the Reign of God.

It needs to involve more than food: abstaining from social media, for example, and exercising self-restraint from what can be overly attractive to the passions – 'the bitter thought, the hasty retort, the angry gesture' (*Principles*, Society of St Francis, Day 27). Have I become addicted to anything – my smartphone, TV, Facebook, critical voices? 'Know thyself', said the Delphic oracle, a dictum that's always been an important aspect of the Life.

The witness of life

From early times some wandered from place to place, never settling anywhere, 'gyrovagues' St Benedict called them, whose lack of stability carried risks. The constant need for something new, different, more appealing – perfect – is addictive and such wanderings can prevent us confronting one from whom we can never escape – ourselves – and from finding God through love and service of others.

During the early Christian era many faced martyrdom for which they prepared by committing to live with a deepening devotion to Jesus. But once persecution diminished, the desert offered another form of martyrdom. Hermits witnessed (which is the meaning of martyr) to their faith through renunciation and the desire to do penance for sins; to pray to overcome evil, give glory through a life wholly dedicated to Godly worship based on Christ's poverty, celibacy and obedience. In Ireland this became known as 'green' martyrdom as distinct from the 'red' martyrdom of those who shed their blood for Christ, or the 'white' of those persecuted for their witness.

Throughout the centuries there have been other forms of solitary life. Julian of Norwich (1343–after 1416), for example, was an 'anchorite', hidden from sight in a cell attached to a church where she could be contacted by those who sought advice or direction and where she dictated the first book written in English by a woman, the *Revelations of Divine Love*.

To live the life of the solitary is to make a conscious decision for 'aloneness' with God and my additional vow of solitude seeks to make concrete my desire for God which becomes the foundation of my active ministry as the contemplative and the active influence and feed each other. (Amma Sue SCL)

'The Desert a City'

Changeless, unmoving power of love,
Guiding, sustaining all,
Drawing, yet leaving free.

Constraining, winning our hearts to love,
Image your life in ours,
Your death our passing through.
(Malling Abbey, Hymn at None)

Three solitaries

Father Bill Kirkpatrick lived in the west London desert of bedsit land. Describing himself as a 'contemplative activator' he spent time early each morning in his chapel beneath the pavement of the Earls Court Road. At night he ministered to rent boys on the streets and in the pubs and clubs of the area, as well as exercising a unique ministry in the early days of HIV/AIDS. Clearly a man of God, we first met when he was Coordinator of Centrepoint, the charity in Soho for homeless young people, where I volunteered. Bill's simple lifestyle and contemplative gaze were obvious and, within six months of each other, we both tested our vocation to the Franciscans.

I not only believe, I know that to be gay ... is a co-creative gift from God to me, offered co-creatively for myself as well as others. This is true of the whole spectrum of human sexuality when not abused or exploited. As a man who happens to be gay, a Christian and a priest, I am called to be a co-creative, co-healing lover of hope, one who is on the side of human dignity and liberty within a freedom confirmed by and through the gospels of love, hope, justice and peace. These actions are affirmed by the Beatitudes, the Magnificat and the Parables of the New Testament – if you like, the rule book for Christians. Therefore, my commitment ... is to be politically active against all that discriminates, dehumanises, de-souls; all that moralises and is judgemental in the name of legalism rather than love. (Kirkpatrick 2005, p. 8of.)

Earlier, Bill had encountered another would-be solitary, Raymond Lloyd – later Br Ramon SSF. Converted as a child to a radical, joyful Christianity (and pacifism), this former Baptist minister had lived with a small community of hermits in Roslin, Scotland. The (ecumenical) Community of the Transfiguration, part-founded by Fathers Roland Walls, Robert Haslam and John Halsey, never numbered more than five living in the manner of the Desert Elders. Initially influenced by the spirituality of Bl Charles de Foucauld (1858–1916), Taizé, and the worker-priest movement, Ramon himself became a Franciscan hermit, writing many popular books on prayer and spirituality.

Solitude's stillness is the place of vision,
Gazing on Beauty, wrapped in silence still,
Sharing the glory of the triune splendour
Learning the meaning of the Father's will.
(Ramon SSF 1989, p. 211)

Apart from having their hearts set on God, what's noticeable about each was their poverty, their radical simplicity and hospitality. Each was aided by a remarkable Anglican contemplative, Mother Mary Clare SLG (1906–1988), who profoundly influenced the development of the solitary life in the Church of England:

> We must learn to wait upon the Spirit of God. As he moves us, we are led into deeper purgation, drawn to greater self-sacrifice, and we come to know in the end the stillness, the awful stillness, in which we see the world from the height of Calvary. (Mary Clare SLG 1993)

Each also owed something to Fr William of Glasshampton SDC (1862–1937) who, in 1918, had been given permission to respond to the Spirit's call to a more contemplative life. As Fr Gilbert Shaw said of him, he 'lived for a recovery of true and primitive monasticism for men as the answer to the crisis of the times' (Shaw 1959). While some came to share in his life and many sought his advice, including Stanley Baldwin, the former prime minister, none stayed. In that he followed Bl Charles de Foucauld who also hoped to develop a contemplative community but was murdered after spending 15 years living alone in the Sahara.

Both apparently failed, but the seeds they sowed eventually grew to bear fruit. Bl Charles inspired the Little Brothers and Sisters of Jesus and Fr William is considered co-founder of the Community of the Servants of the Will of God (CSWG). Glasshampton monastery is now home to brothers of the Society of St Francis seeking a more contemplative life shared, for a time, by their novices and many guests.

> Be content to live an anonymous, unspectacular, misunderstood life. Choose, where possible, those places and jobs where people are oppressed or deprived. Let Christ transfigure the darkness in ourselves and in the world. Let his presence and promise shine like a lamp in a dark place, until the Day dawns and the Daystar arises in our hearts. (Franciscan Hermits of the Transfiguration, *Rule*)

All are now dead, but many others live in ways informed by the wisdom of the desert. Br Harold at Shepherd's Law and the Community of the Servants of the Will of God offer ways where different eremitical traditions meet. Others live unobserved lives among us, but all invite us to consider our calling, their solitude continuing to speak with that stark profundity needed by our church and age.

From solitude to communion

As early as the mid-1850s the call of a sister of the Society of the Holy and Undivided Trinity to a life of almost total solitude was recognized (Allchin 2014, p. 2). More recently a Holy Name sister, living in a hermitage on the north-west coast of Wales, said that like many who live such a hidden way she heard a 'call to the holy', to living 'on the edge'; a liminal home whose walls are thin to the elements, both natural and supernatural. Living in greater at-oneness with nature, our forebears had a clearer awareness of their soul and, in touch with the centre of their being, realized the Divine permeating the world around them.

Few of us live in remote places but the sacramental witness of solitaries who consecrate their lives to God through profound simplicity questions much of our culture. Their courage can inspire us to inhabit solitude and develop our own cell: 'we should make a dwelling place within ourselves', wrote St Francis of Assisi in his *Rule* of 1221, 'where He can stay, He who is the Lord God Almighty, Father, Son, and Holy Spirit'.

Enter into yourself, leave behind all noise and confusion. God speaks to us in the great silence of the heart. Look within yourself and see whether there be some sweet hidden place within where you can be free from noise and argument, where you need not be carrying on your disputes and planning to have your own stubborn way. Hear the word in quietness that you may understand it. (St Augustine, *Sermon* 56.22)

Solitude

Be silent
still
aware.
for there,
in your own heart
the Spirit is at prayer.

Listen and learn
open and find
heart-wisdom
Christ.
(Mother Osyth OSB, Malling Abbey)

'The kingdom of heaven,' said Jesus, 'is like a merchant in search of fine pearls; on finding one pearl of great value, he went and sold all that he had and bought it' (Matt. 13.45). In many ways, those who enter Religious Life are like that merchant and the Life can be thought of as the 'field' where treasure – the unfathomable riches of Christ – lies buried. I'm not suggesting everyone should sell up and enter a hermitage, but I do believe that life contains riches.

> We may ask ourselves what took the fathers into the desert: we may answer constantly – love for God and to do penance for sin. The purpose of the desert is to live by the words of eternal Life.
> (Fr Gilbert Shaw, unpublished talk to SLG)

I encountered my first solitary in 1972 while picking apples at Bede House, a skete or lavra (group of hermits) in the Kentish countryside. Mother Mary Clare SLG and Fr Gilbert Shaw, Warden to the Sisters, had prayed for such a development and it was eventually agreed that the sisters were 'called to go beyond the question of temporary deserts for a few and try to recover for the Church of England the fullness of the contemplative life in a settlement of solitaries' (Allchin 2014, p. 86). In May 1967 Bede House had been blessed by Archbishop Michael Ramsey and five years later, when I was going through a difficult period, my confessor suggested I visit.

The value of the solitary life isn't simply a matter of being alone but of being centred in the desire for God by laying aside distractions, being prepared to feel their loss and to fast from what tempts ear and eye. It's like the white space surrounding printed words; the rest between musical notes; the stillness of the heart between breaths or saying 'no' to busyness.

Loneliness, aloneness and solitude

But solitude can easily be experienced as loneliness. Ultimately, of course, we are alone, known fully only to our Creator whom we encounter through the lens of our soul, that God-given immortal diamond. Aloneness isn't the same as loneliness.

Some are alone by force of circumstance. A partner may have left, died, or never been found, or it can be experienced through being housebound. Closing the door at night and switching off the TV is followed by a dreaded sense of isolation and emptiness – even desolation – which can cause self-obsession, become soul-destroying or leave a person feeling sad or bitter.

But we can embrace the emptiness and turn it into solitude. Familiarity with that place will mean that times of isolation aren't oppressive, for in solitude – the magnificent cell that is the soul's habitation – we can know the wonder of our being and the One who formed and calls us. Here we encounter that positive aloneness needed by contemplatives, the awareness of self in communion with the whole. Mother Mary Clare pointed out that this state can lead a person to a 'deep, heart-searching, listening awareness of the fundamental, crying need of the world' (*Aloneness not Loneliness*, 2010). Instead of seeking to escape aloneness by clinging to another we need to be thankful, abandoning all into God's hands while waiting to be brought through the darkness. To hold everything in Christ whose light would draw goodness out of evil. It's a darkness not to be avoided for, by holding on with faith, hope and love, it can be enlightening.

> If we are to meet the humble Christ, we must descend and go down into the depths of our self and meet him there. This descent is done through our repentance and humility, seeking in prayer and desiring to follow his commandments. In this way we are made whole because our thinking and reflective part, our mind, through the exercise of our will goes down into our heart, our desiring and loving part, and the two are united by the action of God in response to our obedience and repentance. (Colin CSWG 2017, p. 9)

Aloneness and loneliness, solitude and isolation differ. At a time when I faced a life of aloneness, I sensed a need to open my heart with all its confusion and pain to Christ; to pray in that place to him whose love is always there; to repeat and relish his name; praise and thank him for his presence and turn from the darkness to his light. As I've tried to be more centred in him, I know I *need* aloneness at times and to resist distractions (turn off that phone and laptop). Such solitude can be hard for, beneath life's surface, dryness and darkness can be experienced causing some to fear their inner world. But being there is part of the redemptive process of the soul's journey to God whose unapproachable light is veiled in darkness. That can be difficult for those taught that worship is all about joy and praise, but anyone prepared to embark on the integrative, contemplative journey will know – this is the way. And it is a way the church needs to proclaim.

Darkness

Some speak of times when they sense a 'cloud of unknowing' obscuring the presence of God. Everyone goes through times of darkness and confusion which may be part of the way God moves us from being spoon-fed to desire God alone (cf. Eph. 4.13f.). The world may offer distractions, but Christians need at such times (which can come when we least expect them) to express a profound prayer of abandonment to the One upon whom we're utterly dependent. This is the move from self-centredness to trust in God, a hard and risky move, but a further stage of the soul's enfolding in Christ, who takes us through his death and resurrection.

As we grow in our relationship with God, we will experience times of dread, of struggle to be still and peaceful. Times when we bring to our prayers some huge difficulty or sadness in our lives. Times when our faith is tested through a situation not of our own choosing. All we have to do is to trust that God will look after us as we pray. This is to enter truly into the burning fiery furnace which would consume but does not. We must expect that Christ will ... accompany us in our time of affliction. (Christine SLG, 'The Refiner's Fire', *Fairacres Chronicle*, Winter 2019)

Occasionally I've experienced a profound emptiness and need to avoid centring into any sense of despair, knowing that I'm invited to pray into that place where God is hidden, just as Christ entered the darkness of Hades to free those imprisoned there (Acts 2.24; 1 Peter 3.19).

Unseen warfare

As we dive deeper (and at other times) we can be tempted by evil spirits – I don't mean creatures with horns and hoofs, far too obvious, and we'll rarely notice them if we live on the surface of life. Spending time in the silent prayer of longing love can, at some point, lead to feelings of darkness and loss as we draw closer to God and become blind to any realized sense of Presence, just as Christ experienced the absence of his Father on the cross. It's of utmost importance at such times to be accompanied by a discerning spiritual director and, if depression does set in, a therapist.

When Mother Mary Clare pointed out that the hermit stands at the 'point of tension where the love of God and evil meet' she was addressing the place where these powers play out their contest in the heart. Anyone given to the practice of contemplative prayer will be plagued by memories and begin to get bored and tempted by the thought 'does God care?' 'For whose benefit am I doing this?' 'Why bother?' Desert Elders, having parted from the distractions of the 'world', were only too aware of such temptations – negative movements (evil spirits) – which they termed *accidie* and knew they needed to keep the eye of their heart fixed on God.

> The demonic is expressed in an atmosphere which blunts the moral sensibility and makes cross selfishness look like reasonable prudence. All this evil is for Fr Benson personified as Satan as an enemy to be fought, as a deceiver to be unmasked, as a spiritual atmosphere to be resisted. If we wish to demythologise Satan just take care not to underestimate the demonic and weaken our capacity to fight it. (Smith SSJE 1980, p. 91)

This is an aspect of purgation involving waves of temptation and desolation attacking hope, corrupting love and questioning us; 'diabolic attacks' which St Antony of Egypt and others experienced, and not simply exaggerated figments of the imagination. When that happens, solitaries need to reclaim their faith and set their will to possess and be possessed by God. Like them we need to be prepared to stay in that place no matter how empty or filled with discouraging voices it may be, for this is a necessary part of the cleansing process as someone has pointed out, it is normal to experience solitude sometimes as a refuge from other people, and sometimes as a burning fiery furnace.

Those who live intentionally in such places find they're also encountering the heart of the world which speaks into their own. Whether solitaries in Egypt, the Llyn Peninsula in Wales or downtown Manhattan they realize that, in the end, 'our struggle is not against enemies of blood and flesh, but against the rulers, against the authorities, against the cosmic powers of this present darkness, against the spiritual forces of evil in the heavenly places' (Eph. 6.12). They go to the heart of darkness bearing the weapons of light: 'There can be no rest,' wrote Fr Benson SSJE, 'except in proportion to the struggle, no vision except in proportion to the purification of heart, no purification except in proportion as the agony of satanic conflict squeezes out the lifeblood of our corrupt nature' (*Cowley Evangelist*, 1919, p. 205).

At a time when many have given up on the notion of God and forgotten the call to seek 'holiness', the appeal to explore the inner desert and fight the spiritual forces of evil might not be appealing. Yet unless we do those forces can be overwhelming: the call to any form of eremitical life isn't simply for the sake of the individual but the whole body of Christ – indeed, for the sake of the world. Yet the Church often seems unaware of this 'unseen warfare' although many *are* searching for *something*, groping after a variety of spiritualities or trying to practise Mindfulness. But that call which echoed in the heart of Antony continues to resonate, no matter how loud the clamour around us.

Developing our cell

The call to a more contemplative life as we begin to realize God in all things and feel drawn more deeply into that Mystery can come at any time and be difficult to understand. In a society that measures worth by activity, or for people who have grown up with a strong work ethic, such a life can seem self-indulgent. But gradually, it becomes impossible to ignore a longing for places to be alone – with God. This can take many forms – a favourite chair or place set apart, a particular walk or bench in the park. All of us have a need to cultivate such a place – what Russians call our inner *poustinia*, the cell of the heart.

> Do not be anxious about anything. Keep silent, be careful for nothing, give yourself to (reciting the scriptures), sleeping and waking in the fear of God – then you will not fear the attacks of the godless. (Anonymous Desert Elder)

There the long, slow work of the Spirit occurs and we, like every solitary, need to remain faithful to our 'cell'. Gradually I've learned to befriend that solitary place which needs cleansing so that those fruits of the Spirit – love, joy and peace, forbearance, kindness, goodness, faithfulness, gentleness and self-control (Gal. 5.22f.) – can be cultivated. And at its heart is the holy cross, rooted in the earth *and* reaching to heaven with arms embracing the world:

Hidden in the Cross
A heart breaks with joy at the power of your Love
The love of a Lover of Souls
One bringing to each the unspeakable hidden spaces
　of Grace
That which only the Spirit gives
A Grace that forges forgiveness and hope
In the thrust of thorns, the iron nails, and a
　wounding spear
The only sacrifice worthy in the suffering Cross.
(Eileen Marie Ferriot, TSSF)

AFTERWORD

For each one of us, there is a cell,
an intimacy with God
which is ours alone.
An intimacy to inhabit yet to seek and find.
The cell is behind us and within us and before us.
A cell known, and yet to be known;
A place which is also a journey;
A journey which is also a stillness.
An aloneness which is all-one-ness;
A belonging, an at-one-ness.

It will be the place we will recognize
When we come at last
into that longed for presence;
With and within the One who is;
And who is all in all.

For God alone my soul in silence waits ...
(Ps. 62.1)

Sr Pauline Margaret CHN

This sacred 'cell of the heart' needs enfolding in my own 'enclosure' to maintain proper boundaries, even though there will be times when I need to allow others to 'enter'. Giving such 'permission' can help prevent irritation and anger when there's a feeling people are 'breaking in'.

When things go well, when life's full and exciting and there's so *much* to do, it's tempting to feel that spending time there is unnecessary. But it's easy for things to go wrong, even spectacularly wrong. Living on the crest of a wave, the world looking at us with envy, has its dangers, and it's easy to suddenly become the subject of scorn and ridicule. So, when a crisis does come remember that it also offers an opportunity, albeit painful, for a more profound relationship with Christ.

I often reflect how, in our 'instant' culture, we expect to enjoy the good things of life as a right. The quest for happiness and self-fulfilment can be taken for granted, blinding us to the truth that the attainment of God isn't the same as wanting a peaceful, pain-free life; nor must 'spirituality' become confused with pleasant feelings. People like William of Glasshampton remind us that devotional practices alone – methods of meditation or mindfulness practices – as valuable as they may be will not bring us closer to God. What *will* is our loving; our silent, faithful – costly – loving which requires patience leading to *metanoia* and a preference for God alone. The hard way of the cross leads us beyond simply wanting 'felt' experiences to being vulnerable to the divine presence by means of self-denial, abandonment and faithful living out the Divine Will of love.

Two Marys and a John

The Mother of Christ has long been a model for solitaries and all Religious, for Jesus was conceived deep in her heart and, from that sacred space, given to the world. It was Mary who was intimately connected with his human development, enabling her to tell the servants at the wedding feast to do what her Son told them, causing water to be turned into abundant wine (John 2.1–11). Mary's faithfulness, together with the way she 'kept all these things in her heart', gives her a special place in the Christian life.

Jesus commended another Mary (Luke 10.38–42) for wanting to be physically close to him by sitting at his feet. John the Beloved, to whom Jesus entrusted his mother (John 19.26f.), also speaks to the contemplative life for it was he who, resting his head on the Lord's heart (John 13.25), heard its beat. So, if Jesus commended the contemplative life, mustn't the Church?

The solitary shows that God can be found in waste places, and those with the courage to face being alone have helped me face my own wilderness. Christ is to be found there; the Spirit uniting all who are in him both in this world and among the saints, and the Father smiles on our efforts. Rather than being blinded by desert demons we need to look and see the holy ones telling us that the darkness is filled with light, and the stillness can dance.

> Love takes to itself the life of the loved one;
> the greater the love the greater the suffering of the soul,
> the fuller the love, the fuller the knowledge of God;
> the more ardent love, the more fervent the prayer;
> the more perfect the love, the holier the life.
> (Sophrony 1999, pp. 364–5)

3

Silence and Meditation

Prayer and Praise

Be silent, all people, before the Lord;
for he has roused himself from his holy dwelling.
(Zechariah 2.13)

'If God exists, why doesn't he say something?' To those who
ask that question I am tempted to reply: because it's by way
of silence we 'hear' God. The Scriptures record few occasions
when God 'spoke'. Twice God did so creatively and for all time
– once 'in the beginning' (Gen. 1.6) and then at a new beginning when the Word entered our flesh (John 1.1).

> The Father spoke one Word, which was His Son,
> and this Word He always speaks in eternal silence,
> and in silence must It be heard by the soul.
> (Kavanaugh and Rodriguez 1991, p. 21)

We live in a noisy, messy world that often permeates the
Church, which is why many are attracted to quiet places. They
follow Elijah who listened to the sound of sheer silence (1 Kings
19.11f.), leading St John of the Cross to declare: 'What we
need most to make progress is to be silent before this great God
with our appetites and our tongue, for the language he best
hears is silent love' (Kavanaugh and Rodriguez 1991, p. 53).

In silent wonder I've slept in Egyptian deserts under their
starry canopy and realized a Presence both loving and intimate

yet requiring no voice to be 'heard'. Is it because we are of the same stuff of which stars are made that we connect with them? Do they speak of heavenly intimacy just as the seas from which we emerged invite us into the depths?

Through nature I've sensed an at-oneness with all things. Often, I walked through the dark, dank, green lane snaking around the western edge of Hilfield Friary where it had sunk into the Lower Greensand, sometimes climbing up to our wooden hermitage in the overlooking, densely forested hill-side. There a more ancient world opened: as I walked, I would stop to gaze across the vast expanse of the Blackmore Vale and wonder at the beauty of God's intimate handiwork revealed in field and hedgerow, touching my soul and helping me give thanks for the wonder of my own being. But we can connect with that intimacy everywhere, even in the rush of a city – we just need to open our heart and inbreathe divine love uniting us with creation and Creator.

Words are not enough;
only a life indwelt can hold
prayer without ceasing.
(Malling Abbey, *Whittled Words*)

Word into silence

The words to which we attend shape the people we become. In *The Religious Vocation* Fr Benson SSJE wrote that speech

> must be the expression of wisdom in the power of love, as the Word of God is the wisdom of the Father coming forth in the power of the Holy Ghost ... for the word that comes forth from our lips is only the utterance of that which is already found within the heart, for that which is repressed does not cease to be. (2020, p. 293f.)

We also need to take care of what we say (Matt. 12.33f) and the mind in which words are formed needs enfolding in the silence of the heart, the unitive centre of our being where the Spirit prays. To begin each day with heart-silence opens us to God, connecting us to that great ocean of which we're part. Silence can be refreshing: birthed from eternal silence and having to finally leave this world alone, both silence and solitude are ways to cosmic belonginess.

Yet silence can give the impression that God has disappeared. Images and understandings we had might vanish, and we're left with a sense of absence. This can be a necessary development but causes some to reject God; others wait in the darkness as they realize that God is no-thing, yet with patient, loving, trustful waiting they come to a deeper understanding of being held in that ocean of divinity.

Without silence and solitude our humanity is impaired. Br Ramon SSF explored this in *A Hidden Fire* where he recounts what happens in the heart of the solitary as they descend beneath their individuality and encounter a profound sense of belonging to the whole of humanity with all its joy and pain and discover divine Love in and through that calling. 'When I open myself to God in silent adoration,' wrote one solitary:

I have to look inwardly and see myself as God sees me, the weak and sinful person I am, though loved by God 'just as I am'. Union with God must be within that quiet room Jesus spoke of – the interior silence of the soul at prayer. Living the life of a contemplative is not solely for my own spiritual growth for God has given me the gift of being able to listen prayerfully to other people and the strength and courage to communicate His love both by listening to and praying for them. (Mary Vickerage SCL)

Silence is not the absence of noise, but a place to be inhabited. It's in the silent 'prayer of the heart' that we encounter hints and guesses about God and our true selves, the person from whom we cannot escape and with whom we need to compassionately live. Each day we need to return to this deep reality of who we are in Christ – in the eyes of the One who loves us.

In prayer, as in life, the cleansing of the memory and the stilling of an over-active imagination is an integral part of the purgative way. We must remember that suppression is dangerous and can be the cause of spiritual accidie (*listless-ness*) as well as psychological disturbance, but the cleansing that unifies and stills us must come through the uprising of love, the desire to be wholly God's. True silence is to be found in the willingness to be wholly conformed to God's will. (Mary Clare SLG 1972, p. 3)

In *Mole Under the Fence* (Ferguson 2006, p. 127f.), Fr Roland Walls talks about silence as ultimately a 'sacrament of nothing-ness', of complete poverty and death. Where even 'Bible words' need listening to at a deeper level and where poverty is reaching out to be fed: 'Silence is the way in which God has expressed his fullness.' That's the attractive thing about the silence of a Religious house. In silence, says Roland, everything – no matter how small – can be noticed and you know you're sharing life with something even if it's a 'tiny spider'. Does our worship allow for attentive silence?

Recollected living

Such listening is necessary. Most of us exist in a hubbub and it's difficult to reduce its volume to know God's assurance that we, and the world, are beloved. As a sister said, adapting a saying of Abba Moses of Egypt: 'stay in your heart; your heart will teach you everything'.

The early solitaries discovered the necessity of keeping their minds fixed on God, present in every moment, and not becom-ing distracted – by past passions, present anxieties, or future worries. They waited on God, learning to live a 'recollected life', for such recollection is the prelude to contemplation requiring an inner silence guarded by solitude.

The present moment becomes a moment of intense reality to (the one who lives in it): but to most men the present moment is squeezed out of shape ... by the presence of the past, or the future. (Benson SSJE 1927, p. 88)

Living in Christ requires a certain 'stepping back' if we are to know ourselves more clearly. That can be hard in a world where we're encouraged to give fleeting attention, and whole industries have developed to keep us connected and entertained. It's easy to become addicted to the point that distractions blind us to the sacredness of life, and one challenge might be to wean ourselves from whatever prevents us developing and responding to an awareness of God's presence.

A Coptic (Egyptian) monk once pointed out to me that, unlike his homeland where people have known monastics since before Anthony entered the desert, the Reformation severed our relationship with those consecrated to exploring the depths. Yet still the Spirit can be sensed as it flows in places where God is sought: one nun told me that even their agnostic plumber says that something about her Abbey touches him: is he conscious of the scent of those long-forgotten streams?

Inner silence

> Silence is not a thing we make; it is something into which we enter. It is always there ... All we can make is noise.
>
> Mother Maribel CSMV

Contemplation requires developing inner silence. This isn't just about a 'bit of peace and quiet' but a silence that cleanses, which the soul needs to bring us into a right relationship with God so we can enter more deeply into the ocean of God's presence.

As I descend into this soul-silence I am aware of my 'monkey-mind' – the noise and disturbance that has entered me. Then the Spirit brings hidden things to light and provides opportunities for healing. Many will have experienced painful events, and in silence such memories can slowly surface – sometimes after years of being hidden. Such events might be traumatic and it is important not to suppress them again. For this process of attaining holy-wholeness requires patience, trust and, possibly, the aid of a spiritual director and therapist (I know how helpful they can be), as we seek healing in God's loving gaze. And if the Spirit makes me aware of things dark and oppressive, I've learned the importance of gently staying with them, holding myself before God and not running away, for something of importance is being revealed.

The person who prays, maybe someone committed to the life of a hermit, can learn to live at the point of intersection where the Love of God and the tensions and sufferings we inflict on one another meet, and we are held to God's transforming love. (Mary Clare SLG in Schiller 1977, p. 6)

Once, while staying with Religious, I was spending a prayer-time in chapel when a sister came in, began moving furniture and preparing the altar for Mass. She did so gently and quietly, but a little demon awoke and began jumping up and down shouting: 'Why does she have to do that! Can't she see *I'm* trying to meditate? Why disturb *me*!' The demon whined loudly until, I realized, I was giving more attention to him than to prayer; my demanding ego had me in its grip and I'd ignored the invitation to practise detachment.

Attentiveness

Today, many search for practices to make them more centred and still. But for the contemplative, inner silence and stillness aren't ends in themselves, but the means whereby the heart can be focused on loving God and neighbour. Outer silence can help, but it is inner, loving, silence that needs nurturing. That probably means slowing down and not attending to those strident, twittering voices that have a disturbing effect on our inner world as they stir the 'passions' into life. The importance of this 'in-reach' prayer to the development of our humanity indicates that the Church should be supporting and encouraging contemplation with as much, if not more, commitment as it does outreach.

One of the benefits of staying with a specifically monastic community is that they believe in contemplation to the extent of giving their lives to its practice and, hence, to the practice of noticing and wondering. From a piece of carving in the chapel to the song of a bird, shared silence aids internal attention in creating a space where we can be more fully present. But silence can be difficult for some who say they can't cope because they don't know what to 'do': as extroverts, they need action – just 'being' is boring. Yet, when you're alone with your*self*, might the boring bit be ... awareness of 'self'? This led St Augustine to point out that when we come to heaven 'good works' will pass away (*Sermons on the New Testament* 53.5), another reason why, on entering the house of Mary and Martha, Jesus said that Mary, by sitting at his feet, had chosen the 'better part'. Not that what Martha was doing wasn't of value, just that Mary's attentiveness was better and wouldn't be taken away.

The Rhythm of Prayer

Prayer is the expression
of our poverty:
having nothing of our own we wait upon God,
empty, silent, dependent;

of our chastity:
held in the love of Christ,
we rejoice to be with God who is all to us;

of our obedience:
we give ourselves in total surrender,
desiring only God's will in all things.
(CSC, *Rule*)

Many 'pray as they go', fitting it in when possible, but Religious Life taught me the importance of developing a disciplined rhythm independent of mood. Mother Millicent SPB said the Church needed to be encouraged on this way of the 'cross of faith' which will involve at least prayer in the morning and evening together with times of silence and solitude.

Details will depend on circumstances, just as some Orders are called to give more time to prayer than others, but for all the 'Opus Dei' – God's working – is primary. We find space for things we regard as important, so how about 10, 20 – even 30 – minutes of loving silence each day when we can simply be open to the Spirit? Of course, there's too much to 'do'! But maybe – *maybe* – setting aside time each day for meditation will help develop an integrated life, especially important for those charged with pastoral care.

Called into living prayer

> If Christ lives in us, then he prays in us, and our chief concern should be to provide him a place where he can pray. How good if he can say of us, 'This is my body in which I can pray, through which I can make contact with souls, into whom and through which channel I can pour my love, which I can even break, if need be, for the salvation of the world.' But he waits for our 'fiat' before taking possession.
>
> Mother Maribel CSMV, *The Stations of the Cross*

For almost two centuries, Religious Life has helped Anglicans realize the centrality of prayer. The Rule of the Community of the Transfiguration states: 'Your vocation is none other than the call of God ... who wills you to live to his praise and glory.' In the end, that's the vocation of every Christian but this Life, with prayer its heartbeat, offers immense insights into how our life can reveal God's glory. For prayer is an act of humility asking us to be open and honest about ourselves as we come before our Creator.

Prayer has been described as 'turning our whole mind, our whole being, towards God ... True prayer is the one-ing of our will with the will of God. This takes the whole of our attention but by it, God may use us as instruments through which his power may work in the present to remedy the past and heal the future' (Shaw 1973, unpublished paper). It isn't simply an act we perform but a way of living (1 Thess. 5.17).

Slowly, and with help, I began to relish the way prayer concerns this reaching out to God in faith, hope and love. Gradually the eye of my heart opened to its need for *metanoia*, my awareness of the needs of the world deepened, and I realized a sense of inner joy – even in times of pain. To be fully human involves this opening to God, which is why the more I prayed the more I found it became something I *needed* and the more I *wanted* to pray, no matter how difficult it might be or what I might discover. 'Prayer', as one sister said, 'concerns immersing yourself in God and focusing your whole attention on him.'

Who may sing the song of Love?
Those only who give all, without reserve, hold nothing back,
'tis they who know the joy, the quickening pain of Love;
'tis they who taught by adoration hold the Heart of Love
and touch all loveless hearts to life by giving Love.
(Shaw 2000, p. 60)

Beyond beginnings

As our spiritual life develops, it is bound to be a progress out of multiplicity and turmoil into simplicity and unity. It tends to develop in us a fixity of gaze upon God and, as we gaze, particular things drop off; they seem to matter no longer. We desire only more and more complete surrender, in order that we may keep clear a channel through which Christ may pray.

Mother Maribel CSMV, *The Stations of the Cross*

This silence is a response to the fact that we not only need times when noise ceases but also times when the inner life can flourish. Developing a stillness when we are not distracted by a thousand and one things is the beginning, but meditation can move us further into that Mystery hidden in darkness and realized in silence.

As a Franciscan I shared in five periods of formal prayer and an hour or more of personal prayer each day when I discovered new ways to pray. But what mattered most was simply being there (even if I fell asleep), offering my heart to God, keeping it swept clean and giving it as much attentiveness as I could. The rest I entrusted to God. As a Precious Blood sister said: 'Don't test prayer by how you consequently feel. Yet when God *does* touch the heart, there's a way he moves us.'

> We must remember that all prayer which is true prayer represents the touch of God on the soul. When the soul in grace turns to God in prayer, when the divine life rises up within and echoes back the life and love of God. Because all true prayer represents the work of grace within, therefore the approach to prayer depends not so much on any ordered process as on the reality of humility. (Fr Lucius Cary SSJE, in Colin CSWG 2017, p. 53)

The hidden Christ

Almost from the beginning some Anglican Religious came to recognize that being 'catholic' involves understanding how God calls through other faiths. Fr Benson wrote that 'We must see varied manifestations of the divine goodness' and while '(t)hat essence … is manifested completely in the person of Christ' he admits that '(a)ll the varied surroundings glow with traces of the divine glory' (Benson SSJE 2020, p. 201). This early recognition developed as other faiths were encountered where communities became established, not least in India. The fruit of those encounters meant some opened to the wisdom others found threatening, but which has enriched the Church through the lives of Religious such as Father Slade SSJE and Father Bill Lash CPSS (former Bishop of Mumbai). In time I discovered this and, along with others, engaged in creative dialogue with a number of Buddhist monks.

Liturgy

Mary treasured all these words and pondered them in her heart. The common life of our Community is centred on the worship of God through the Eucharist, the Daily Office and personal prayer. This is its first work and from this all else flows. (CSMV, *Rule*)

God-centred worship is our primary call. It's not that if we don't worship God, we won't worship anything – quite the contrary. But to be fully human involves worship; it's in our DNA. I don't mean God is a demagogue demanding adulation; rather, our heart needs to be set on that communion of divine Persons in whose image we are created (Gen. 1.27) and who desire to draw us into their glory. Anything less risks us being misled.

'Liturgy' means a duty performed, so when the chapel bell rang, and we gathered to sing God's praises we were not only doing what early Christians did (Acts 2.46f.) but engaging in a formative act. I found myself nourished by psalms and scriptures no longer obscured through the fog of Tudor English or complicated chant and learned to pray through contemplative plainsong written by monastics to enable the words to be carried into the heart of God. It echoes the worship of the ages, a musical icon giving expression to the Word (Christ) present in words. Choirs today could learn much from traditional and modern monastic singing. Dom Xavier Perron OSB has written an excellent introduction to the importance of plainsong in the Divine Office in *Oneness: The Dynamics of Monasticism* (Platten 2017, chapter 8).

Through shared, holistic liturgy involving body, mind and spirit we are drawn into the life of the Trinity. As my experience of communal prayer developed, I realized that more was happening than just the coming together of individuals, each intent on their private prayer. Here was a growing union of hearts and minds focused on God as we worshipped the One who is a Trinity in Unity; whose creation realizes itself most perfectly through common acts of praise (Ps. 104).

Liturgical worship is meant to reflect our vocation to common union rather than individualism and this seems exemplified by monastic (a word indicating unified purpose) worship, expressing in a profound way the prayer of Christ. Worship opens a door by which Divine energies flow through the created order so it can become one with its Creator.

When I come to pray I am putting myself as it were into the midst of a great stream and volume of prayer and loving worship, which goes up before God from the whole company of heaven and from the Church on earth all over the world. (Raynes CR 1959, p. 60)

The beauty of holiness

To worship God is an act of sanctifying humility, placing us in an attitude of awe towards the object of reverence. Some say they worship football but when the object is the Creator, the One who entered our flesh, our suffering and death, then it has the power to raise us into divinity and ignoring that belief does nothing to aid our common humanity.

To the place of your choosing
   I come
emptied of all but desire to know
even as I am known

Without words
in the silence of love

my unlikeness yields to your like
your quickening touch penetrating
every fibre vibrating its
'yes'
to the making
One.
(Mother Osyth OSB, Malling Abbey)

God's transforming humility is celebrated in every Eucharist – the descent of Divinity into the things of earth, even the lowest parts – affirming God's union with us. The mingling of the wine of the ageless kingdom with the water of time-bound creation in the chalice of salvation is the means whereby God shines through a broken body. Coming just as we are, gathering our desires into a simple yearning for communion with our Creator, we are one with saints and angels in their great song of praise.

Liturgy requires a contemplative act involving humbly *listening* to each other and I learned that if I couldn't hear others then I was being too dominant – just listen! Speed and rhythm must blend. Liturgy isn't a solo performance but a sharing in the prayer of Christ's mystical Body which can unite us in divine, Eucharistic love.

All Religious affirm the centrality of the Eucharist, the Rule of the Society of the Precious Blood recognizing that 'This sacrifice of praise and intercession is continued throughout the day, especially in the recitation of the Divine Office, in the Watch before the Blessed Sacrament, and in times set aside for silent prayer and contemplation.'

In corporate worship each member's personal experience of dependency upon the Holy Spirit should be multiplied, since in the communion of the Holy Spirit each prays in and through the others. We must ensure, therefore, that the individual members of the choir are not trying to superimpose their own patterns of private prayer onto the common worship, since this would distort the communion of the Spirit.
(Gregory CSWG 1983, p. 24)

But it is not only monastics who declare that prayer is their priority. A sister from one of the 'active' Orders explained how she had always wanted to serve Christ and had been trained for mission by a society that *said* prayer was important but, in practice, was often squeezed out by work. Eventually she looked for somewhere mission flowed *from* prayer and, through her present community, had spent a lifetime praying *and* serving in the UK and overseas.

Corporate silence

One of the most powerful times of corporate prayer I experienced with the Franciscans occurred when we spent half an hour, or an hour, in corporate silence. It could be boring and sometimes others' conflicts were felt, but there were moments when you were aware of a deep at-oneness aiding the building of community in profoundly important, yet unobvious, ways.

Religious Life shows that, rather than being something *extra*-ordinary which can feel as if it is done for the primary benefit of attendees, worship needs to be woven into the warp and woof of life. Instead of 'going to a service', each day was expressed through worship aided by standing, sitting, kneeling, all allowing the whole body to pray. That profound bow at the 'Glory be' humbles us before the Trinity in whose presence we live; making the sign of the cross unites us with the crucified, and sitting aids praying the psalms. As one contemplative said: 'both bowing in chapel and digging in the enclosure aid a creative life'.

Contemplative worship

I still yearn for contemplative liturgy. Apart from that offered by the Quakers, parish worship often seems a form of 'Family Service' leading me, when I was a parish priest, to create a Saturday evening Contemplative Liturgy. With chairs arranged around the altar we began with recorded music and Lighting of the Lamps which opened a simplified Evening Prayer: gently recited psalms; a reading ending in silence; the Canticle and Gospel – abbreviated, if necessary – and no sermon but more silence in which to share reflections. This concluded with a longer silence from which flowed the Intercessions and exchange of the Peace before standing around the altar for the Eucharistic Prayer and Communion and another long period of silence before the dismissal. It wasn't just adults that liked to come – children were also usually present.

> Make me all love
> that I may be all prayer
> that one with you in love
> I may pray the prayer
> of your life, your passion,
> your death and resurrection
> for the whole world.
> (Malling Abbey)

Intercession

All worship requires the gift of our whole being. Setting a table, driving a car, or using a laptop can all be done to God's greater glory and every act offered can be an intercession: 'the total gift of the heart is prayer', said Fr Gilbert Shaw (*Prayer*, 1973).

> Intercession is not words but a life: it is the offering of our-selves, our souls and bodies, to God, that His Will may be done in and through us. It expresses itself in the gold of hard work, the frankincense of prayer, and the myrrh of suffering. We can never be without one of the three; and it is for our Lord to choose which at any time He will accept from us.
> (Community of the Holy Family, *Rule*)

In the end, the most important prayer we can offer is that for our 'enemies', a profound act involving the redemption of Satan – 'the one who opposes'. Such intercession reflects Christ's command to love those who oppose us and, ultimately, requires us to take the light of Christ into the place of deep darkness where a struggle with the cosmic powers of this present age occurs (cf. Eph. 6.10f.).

A sister of Burnham Abbey says that intercession (meaning to 'go between' on behalf of another) involves developing a compassionate heart as part of that *metanoia* which helps change the world. It opens a channel between heaven and earth and involves facing our own brokenness and weakness.

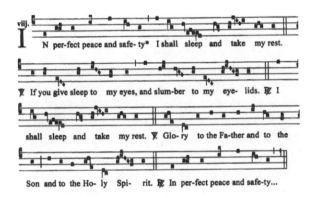

viij.

IN per-fect peace and safe- ty* I shall sleep and take my rest.

℣ If you give sleep to my eyes, and slum-ber to my eye- lids. ℟ I

shall sleep and take my rest. ℣ Glo-ry to the Fa-ther and to the

Son and to the Ho- ly Spi- rit. ℟ In per-fect peace and safe-ty...

From 'Night Prayer', Malling Abbey

The Divine Office

Almighty Father,
inflame our hearts with your Holy Spirit,
that we may pray the Office
with attention and devotion,
for the benefit of those for whom we pray
and to the glory of your Son,
Jesus Christ our Lord. Amen.
(CSMV, based on a prayer before Lauds)

The Opus Dei concerns our participation in God's work, giving the Benedictines one of their mottos – *Ora et labora* (Prayer and work). Work *can* be prayer, for we are invited to do everything to the greater glory of God and the Benedictine Rule even says that 'the vessels of the monastery' need to be treated as the 'sacred vessels of the altar' (*Rule*, chapter 31).

Pray without ceasing

The Desert Elders understood that prayer isn't simply something done when we're moved, but a means whereby the whole of life can express our at-oneness with God. It isn't easy to live with this 'constant recollection of the unseen world' (SSF, *Principles*, Day 14) but, in noting the psalmist's observation 'seven times a day do I praise you' (Ps. 119.164), the Elders developed a rhythm of Offices filled with psalms and readings reflecting the dynamics of Godly time that offered a way of living Paul's injunction to pray without ceasing (1 Thess. 5.16f.). The Offices are extensions of that great Eucharistic 'sacrifice of prayer and praise', reminders that the whole of life is to be lived 'eucharistically', thankfully, in the eternal prayer of Christ who invites us to share in his Heart's intercession for the world.

Sadly, most of us can't stop to pray seven times each day (Muslims put many Christians to shame), but we do need to develop means for expressing union with God. We could intersperse our day with moments of prayer; over 50 years ago I taught myself this simple consecration which, now, emerges from my heart as I awake:

All glory be to Thee, my God, +
for thou art One, all Holy God, very Love.
I herewith renew the offering of myself to Thee
in union with that supreme offering
of Jesus Christ my Lord. Amen.

After leaving community I fasted from the Office until my desire for this ancient spiritual workout became too great and

I returned to exercises from its rich menu. Most of us find our initial fervour dissipates, and it's then we need to settle down to the real work of prayer beneath the passions. A commitment, not based on passing emotional highs, but the need for deep inner conversion.

The sanctification of time

In giving conscious attention to God at different times Religious Life is shaped by the rhythms of the sacred – and natural – seasons; of feasts, fasts and Ordinary Time (an excellent introduction to 'Daily Prayer in the Life of the Church' can be found in *The Daily Office*, SSF, p. 677f.). Some will pray the Offices so they can live with an awareness of themselves as part of that creation which continuously sings with joy. For some, therefore, this also involves prayer in the silent hours of the night.

Keep watch, dear Lord,
with those who work, or watch, or weep this night,
and give your angels charge over those who sleep.
Relieve the anxious, comfort the lonely, give rest to the weary,
pity the afflicted, strengthen the fearful, relieve the depressed,
soothe the suffering, tend the sick, free the addicted,
protect the homeless, give courage to carers,
guard those in danger, enfold the dying,
grant peace to the departed,
and all for your love's sake. Amen.
(Based on a prayer of St Augustine of Hippo)

I recall joining the Sisters of the Love of God at Bede House for the Night Office (Matins) at 2 a.m. and finding that silent, thin, time when the stars, like the psalms we sang, shone brightly and had a solitary freshness that seemed to pierce the darkness and connect with the whole of creation. If you find it hard to sleep, or wake in the middle of the night, try joining those praying this Office.

LAUDS

I rise to greet You
this new day,
'tho night still covers me.

I open my heart
and sing Your praise,
'tho night still holds me.

And though the mists
still swirl around,
the night begins to brighten;

and then my heart
does fill with joy,
for night no longer blinds me.

Lauds (Morning Prayer) takes us into the emergence of light as we 'pass-over' into day with a song of praise – 'Come, let us sing to the Lord' (Ps. 95.1) – offered even in times of darkness and despair. I don't often awake singing for joy, and getting up early is rarely easy, especially if you're alone – what's the point? So, I try to recall that the ringing of my alarm clock is an invitation to begin a new day with a divine Lover who wants to lead me into life, and not just an insistent call to leave my cosy bed. And then I sing hymns left to us by the early Christian poets, many translated by John Mason Neale, founder of the Society of St Margaret:

Do though, O Christ our slumbers wake;
Do thou the chains of darkness break;
Purge thou our former sins away,
And in our souls new light display.
(*English Hymnal*, 53)

Later, Terce (third Hour) recalls the descent of the Holy Spirit on the apostles (Acts 2); Sext (sixth Hour) creates a pause in the middle of the daylight hours so we can reflect on God's handiwork. As we move into the afternoon, None (ninth Hour) is a reminder of Christ's Passion and Death, while Vespers (Evening Prayer) celebrates the fading of light and – according to Judeo-Christian understanding – the beginning of a new day as lamps are lit (Gen. 1.3). Finally, Compline (Night Prayer) delivers us into darkness and places us with Christ who lay in the tomb, leading us to say: 'Into your hands, O Lord ✢, I commend my spirit' (cf. Ps. 31.5).

The Office is meant to inform and mould: it doesn't depend on how we are feeling, nor is it determined by what we choose, but takes us into a dynamic sanctified by God. That's why Offices shouldn't be run together (*Customary*, Society of the Sisters of Bethany, 2008, private publication); praying them is less about fulfilling an obligation than enfolding the one who prays, and that for which they pray, into the prayer of Christ.

With the rhythm of daily time (*chronos*) the Office opens us to sacred time (*kairos*) with its seasons of waiting, preparation and incarnation; of fasting, suffering and resurrection joy, wonder and Spirit-enabled renewal, until we affirm our incorporation into Trinitarian life in Ordinary Time, all revealed in the lives of saints who weave throughout. Religious Life is focused into these dynamics affirming that we are both of this world and citizens of the New Age.

Praise and prayer constitute the atmosphere in which the brothers and sisters must strive to live. They must endeavour to maintain a constant recollection of the presence of God and of the unseen world. An ever-deepening devotion to Christ is the hidden source of all their strength and joy. He is for them the One all-lovely and adorable, God incarnate, crucified and risen, whose love is the inspiration of service and the reward of sacrifice. (SSF, *Principles*, Day 14)

Unadorned liturgy

Though it's many years since I was released from my vows, I'm still drawn to places inhabited by Religious. They have been at the forefront of developing worship with a freshness which isn't dependent on archaic language that can obscure meaning: 'The unadorned Liturgy of these places speaks without the need for frills,' observed a Benedictine nun. It offers a well plunging into God's love, the devotion flowing from it enriching and refreshing because it involves people consecrated to celebrate (hopefully) in unity. No matter how varied their lives (and how annoying they might find each other), they seek to worship with one voice to glorify the one God and Father of our Lord Jesus Christ (cf. Rom. 15.5f.).

I can no longer share in a daily Eucharist but, as an extension of that Liturgy, the Office allows Christ to pray in and through that prayer and, although usually alone, I recall myself belonging to the whole Body of Christ on earth and in heaven: somewhere, someone also prays with me.

Ad gloriam Dei in eius voluntate ('To the glory of God in the doing of his will')

That motto of the Society of the Sacred Mission reminds me that prayer is for God's glory. Some are fortunate in being able to create an oratory (chapel) from a spare room or shed, but I simply place an icon and candle on the floor where I kneel. Anywhere can be consecrated through the persistence of prayer: 'these stones that have echoed thy praises are holy ...' (*New English Hymnal*, 208).

Although not everyone can pray the Offices some devise their own: they may simply say: 'O God, make speed to save me; + O Lord, make haste to help me' (cf. Ps. 40.13), choose a psalm and reading from those given, offer intercessions and pray the Our Father.

For the sake of the world

We also celebrate for the sake of God's world. It's not a matter of me praying my own prayer, but about redeeming life's messiness: self-pride is punctured (Ps. 119.71); anger at enemies turns to trust in God (Ps. 124); concern for the evil in my heart becomes faith in the One who is my salvation (Ps. 140) ... the whole Office is a form of intercession.

> There is me, myself, the person who prays, who is alienated from God: a 'sinner', one who has fallen short of the glory of God and sees in the face of the Lord's majesty his own unworthiness. And in between these two – the majestic God and the sinner – there is *eleison*, 'mercy', the loving kindness of our God. That is the basic theological fact that our whole life is to realise: God in Christ reconciling the world to himself in us and through us day by day; and *that* is the life of prayer. (Mary Clare SLG 1972, p. 17)

Praying the Office is an exercise in uniting ourselves with God through a daily workout demanding our whole attention as we join in a universal process of reconciliation. Religious witness to the fact that there's a better way than that offered by our culture of persuasive capitalism driven by succeeding, accumulating, winning; a culture where nationalism pretends to be patriotic, merit casts many aside, and ambition, promotion and my-way is the path trod. Religious Life affirms that of greater importance is cooperation for the common good and active compassion for those in need. What, then, might we learn from those who, for centuries, have given their lives to worship?

- Presenting ourselves before God with humility, we recognize the majesty of the One to whom we pray, asking Christ to pray through us.
- Recollection is fundamental as we pray: 'May all the words of this prayer be acts of pure love ... adoration ... thanksgiving ... sanctification ... trust and surrender to your holy Will.'

- With thanksgiving, our prayer can be offered for a particular need.

- In attentive, loving confidence, the words we sing/speak need to emerge from the heart – we mustn't rush but pray the psalms and readings. And, even if we're alone, our prayer is best spoken aloud.

The Psalms

Your love, O Lord, forever will I sing;
from age to age my mouth will proclaim your faithfulness.
(Psalm 89.1)

Since about the fourth century, the Psalms, the 'prayer-book of the Bible', have been foundational to the monastic tradition and make up more than two thirds of its Office. In praying them I realize they express the theme that faith in God's will brings life, gradually becoming a catalyst for changing the heart. They provide a hidden reservoir that feeds deeper faithfulness and focus the essence of prayer.

They provide a resource for recognizing a greater unity with creation, something that may be easier in the green of the country than a city's greyness. But I try to open my eyes to see the wonder of God in all things – even that weed bravely growing in the broken pavement – for all created things express wonder at their Creator.

Make me understand the way of your commandments
that I may meditate on your marvellous works.
(Ps.119.27)

For the Desert Elders, they were the means of praying with
and in Christ using words that helped form him (1 Cor. 2.16).
These were the verses he meditated on, scriptures he heard and
hymns he sang so were learned by heart, and formed the bulk
of their prayer. What matters is how attentively and lovingly
they are prayed, for while we can be physically present our
heart-attention can be far away. The speed at which we pray,
the silence held after readings – all aid recollected prayer.

Gradually I learned to 'chew' on the words, letting them
nourish me as I allowed them to inhabit and purify my heart
where they offer a means of intercession. Contemporary
translations allow them to speak to our understanding while
enabling prayer, or they can descend into the heart where each
wants to reveal deeper meaning and, like the poetic form they
use, expand awareness. They will sing in the soul if you let
them, even more so if a simple chant can be on the lips.

I love them because they express penitence, praise and wonder. And, yes, frustration, anger and despair without which
verses I might not include any negative feelings. Some were
written as the pilgrim joyfully 'went up' to Jerusalem; others
we can learn so they are on our lips when we die – de profundis
– 'out of the depths I cry to you, O Lord ...' (Ps. 130.1).

Like the readings they mirror the immense complexity of life
– its pain and pleasure, joy, sorrow, hope and fear – pointing
to the way that he who humbled himself, descending into the
realm of hades, has raised us into resurrection life, his sacrifice
nourishing and offering hope.

O God, whose love is without measure:
    out of the depths of my own creatureliness and yearning
    I call out to you.
Out of your own immense depths of power and mystery
    you call to me.

Enable me to enter into the beginnings
   of the secrets of your love,
   and let the poor stream of my life
   flow into the immensity of your being.
(Ramon SSF 1991, p. 75)

4

The Monastic Way

And Contemplative Living

Uphold me according to your promise, that I may live,
and let me not be put to shame in my hope.
(Psalm 119.116, the 'Suscipe' sung at
Profession in monastic vows)

Monasticism took time to reawaken in the Anglican Communion. After some initial attempts, Benedictine life emerged
from seeds planted in 1863 at Llanthony, near Capel-y-ffyn
in the Black Mountains of Wales. Three years later a few
men set sail to evangelize the Orange Free State in Southern
Africa believing this would best be done in the context of
prayer, poverty and a common life. This led the group to name
themselves The Brotherhood of St Augustine after the great
fourth-century North African monk. While the Brotherhood
no longer exists, the cave they first inhabited is regarded as a
sacred site and place of pilgrimage.

Many do not quite understand monasticism. Priestly life,
yes, and possibly 'sisters of mercy' – they do good works. But
monks? Or nuns? All that silence and solitude, isn't it a bit ...
selfish? Isn't it better to get out there and *do* something? Yet
God still calls to a life where prayer is central because it forms
and informs the rest, and some know they *need* to be given
to God through this way whose very existence, lived for God
alone, can make others feel uncomfortable.

The life developed from the desire of the Desert Elders for

support by sharing aspects of life, thus enabling that loving community understood by the first Christians as revealing the nature of God. They knew it was necessary to focus their lives into God so sought to strip themselves of whatever got in the way. To modern society, filled with distractions – smartphone games, second-rate TV, celebrity culture and all the rest – this radical alternative offers challenging wisdom, and many have been influenced by its evangelizing witness to the power of Christ-centred faith in creating a better world.

One of the appeals of monasticism is that its norms and values are clear – it presents a focused way to live the gospel and a defined way to grow in faith. It gently challenges our tendency to self-absorption and self-determination, showing the richness of a life lovingly lived for God and the benefit of others. It is, as one Religious said, 'the only way I know by which I can offer the whole of myself to God'.

It also questions the greed and desire for 'more' and 'the latest fashion' that is ruining our planet, while countering our busy-ness through a balanced life of prayer, study, work and rest; rest that reflects what happened on the seventh day – God stopped. What is this life if, full of care, we have no time to stand and stare? (W. H. Davies, 'Leisure'). When did you last rest, properly, without having your attention constantly occupied and energized with no time to assimilate, reflect and just *be*?

The Monastic Call

In those days John the Baptist
appeared in the wilderness of Judea, proclaiming,
'Repent, for the kingdom of heaven has come near.'
(Matthew 3.1)

There was a time I felt called to this life and knocked at its door. Although it wasn't right for me to enter, I realize how it offers important insights into living with greater recollection – mindfully, *heart*fully. The hiddenness of monasticism is intended to act as salt (Matt. 5.13) and yeast (Matt. 13.33). Thus, to an age whose mantra is 'be yourself', its emphasis on Christ's teaching that by letting go of your-self (Matt. 16.24–28) you gain life, is not only counter-intuitive but necessary. It is an antidote to the dominance of that overweening ego realized in the demagogues of ours and every age, offering ways to let Christ shine: yet, having said that, even Religious can live in deep darkness. No one is perfect but God alone (cf. Matt. 5.48).

A spiritual guide

Anyone journeying this way will know the importance of having a 'good shepherd', a spiritual director who can guide them; the value of a 'spiritual father/mother' in whom to confide has long been recognized.

It is easy for the roles and duties of clergy (and others) to take over and for them to forget their primary, personal call to God. They, like all of us, will benefit from meeting with someone to whom they can be accountable and who will make sure they are keeping the eye of their heart fixed on Godly love. It is difficult, and sometimes dangerous, to make this journey without such a guide, easy to simply stop at a rest-house along the way and decide to make that home; cease listening to the call to divine union.

The eternal Sabbath

Of course, along the way there is always need of that 'Sabbath rest' which reflects the life to come. When I was about to join the Franciscans, I remember telling a hermit that I would have three weeks holiday each year and naively asking how long she had: 'Holiday, for a hermit?' she replied. 'No, I don't think so...'

While it is right to enjoy times of rest, we need to remember that our relationship with God continues ... even when we reach retirement age. We might rest in God, but prayer needs to go on until, God willing, we cease from much of the 'doing' and give more attention to being consciously present to God. You can't 'retire' from being a Religious (or priest – or Christian), for this journey of conversion continues until we attain the vision of God. Benedict's teaching 'keep death daily before your eyes' (*Rule*, chapter 4) reminds us that we need to live with a constant awareness of God's presence; we aren't to split life into the sacred and secular, active and contemplative, physical and spiritual; all is to be done to God's glory (1 Cor. 10.31).

Monastic Guidelines

If you think you are wise in this age,
you should become fools so that you may become wise.
For the wisdom of this world is foolishness with God.
(1 Corinthians 3.18–19)

Religious Life is aided by guidelines (Rules) intended to help gospel living and those of many Anglican Orders were primarily shaped by two.

Rule of Saint Augustine

Following the example of the Jerusalem community (Acts 4.32–35) the purpose of this short Rule, written c. 397, was to express how Christians might overcome self-centredness and live in love and service of God and neighbour. Almost 1,500 years before Karl Marx, Augustine rejected private ownership, offering a way that would enable both rich and poor to benefit from a common life. Clothing was shared, chastity embraced, conflicts to be quickly resolved and prayer central: 'When you pray to God in psalms and songs, the words spoken by your lips should also be alive in your hearts' (Ch. 2.3).

About 150 years later, St Benedict wrote a Rule that eventually became the norm for most Western monastics and, in what follows, RB stands for the Rule of Saint Benedict while the numbers indicate the chapters and paragraphs of that Rule.

Rule of Saint Benedict

I still recall sitting in the Refectory at Nashdom Abbey and first hearing this Rule read. Comprising 73 chapters, it begins by inviting the person to 'listen carefully ... with the ear of your heart', and to aid that internal listening the life was enfolded in exterior silence. It offers a way 'back to God from whom you have drifted' for anyone 'ready to give up (their) own wills ... to do battle for Jesus'. Containing 'nothing harsh, nothing burdensome' it is a call to those who 'yearn for life', who 'wish to dwell in God's tent' inviting them to turn away from evil and do good.

To aid this, Benedict says he is setting out to 'establish a school for God's service' by 'faithfully observing God's teaching' (RB Prologue). Talk about being at 'school' might be unappealing, but think of it as a way of learning: 'Never drawing back from our discipleship but persevering until death in his teaching ... we shall have part in Christ's sufferings by our patience and deserve also to have part in his Kingdom' (RB Prologue).

In that 'school' the place of the Abbot receives much attention. While they have a leadership role they need to listen to their community as they guide the monks to 'remember what is written: seek first the kingdom of God and his justice, and all these things will be given you as well' (RB 2). In a memorable line Benedict says we should 'prefer nothing to the love of Christ' (RB 4.21) for 'it is love that impels them to pursue everlasting life' (RB 5).

One of his early lessons concerns twelve 'steps' on the ladder of humility by which the Elders taught we might climb to heaven (RB 7). Thirteen chapters are then devoted to praying the Divine

Office (RB 8f.) followed by instruction on community discipline and the role of 'officers'. Benedict's practical guidance is often apparent, not least when he says that 'Overindulgence should be avoided, lest anyone experience indigestion' (RB 39), and I can't help but think he had a smile on his lips when telling the brothers not to read the book of Kings before going to bed (RB 42) 'for it will not be good for those of weak understanding'. Perhaps we might question whether reading a passionate novel or listening to a political debate last thing at night will aid sleep ...

Like Augustine, Benedict points to the evils of private ownership, saying that manual labour is to be undertaken by everyone, for 'idleness is the enemy of the soul' (RB 48). Following this he deals with the matter of monastic hospitality (RB 53) insisting that 'all guests who present themselves are to be welcomed as Christ'; they are God's gifts enabling the exercise of the sacred duty of hospitality, a duty that continues to this day and informs a Christian understanding of the place of the stranger in our midst.

Then, towards the end, he writes that just as there's 'a wicked zeal of bitterness which separates from God and leads to hell, so there is a good zeal which separates from evil and leads to God and everlasting life. This, then, is the good zeal which members must foster with fervent love: they should each try to be the first to show respect to the other.' They aren't to pursue what they judge good for themselves, 'but what they judge better for others ... let them prefer nothing whatever to Christ, and may Christ bring us all together to everlasting life' (RB 72).

One of the reasons I value monastic life is because it reminds me of the need to continue to grow in every aspect of faith, otherwise I'll atrophy. We're meant to: 'come to the unity of the faith and of the knowledge of the Son of God, to maturity, to the measure of the full stature of Christ' (Eph. 4.13). That's the fruit of the Spirit's workings as we open ourselves to the love of God: once that begins to take root, we are invited to abandon ourselves to the perfect love of God with deepening faith and hope that our hearts will continually be filled with that same love, with the Spirit of God.

As the Rule concerns how to live together it appealed to the fragmented society of Benedict's age, one like our own. Recognizing the need to be patient with weakness he says we must strive to live 'in obedience with each other'; and then makes this important statement:

> Let them not follow their own good but the good of others. Let them be charitable towards their brothers with pure affection. (RB 72)

Why is all this important? Because observance of the Rule 'can show that we have some degree of virtue and the beginnings of monastic life ... which will lead ... to the very heights of perfection' (RB 73).

The place of Scripture

Scripture informs the whole of monastic (and Religious) life and meditating on it is central, as it needs to be for all Christians. Whether by using a form of Benedictine *Lectio Divina*, being washed by psalms and readings in the Office or using the imagination to enter a passage, whoever steeps themselves in Scripture will be nurtured. Wrestling with the words as Jacob wrestled with God (Gen. 32.24f.) is creative, informing both prayer and life, for Religious have long known that: 'intellectual honesty and contemplative openness belong together in our life with Scripture' (*The Rule of the Society of St John the Evangelist*, chapter 20).

Anglican monastics

From Canterbury to Winchester, Worcester to Durham, many ancient English cathedrals were founded as centres of Benedictine life. Its charism has informed church and nation in subtle ways; from a Liturgy requiring the daily celebration of Morning and Evening Prayer, to its charism, not least its vows, Benedictine life has helped shape the English. While the

Reformation ripped it out, echoes continued through cathedral worship, the collegiate life of Oxbridge and a few subsequent attempts to develop community living.

However, when efforts were made to reintroduce the life many were extremely opposed – even more so to the introduction of contemplative communities. That's sad: for when I look at the vibrancy of the Church in places like Egypt, I see it's largely due to the continuing centrality of monasticism. Though we now have several communities shaped by Benedict's Rule, most Anglicans are probably unaware of the important work of monastics like Dom Gregory Dix OSB of Nashdom whose book *The Shape of the Liturgy* is still regarded as a major contribution in that field of study.

It was to that monastery a small group of American Episcopalians went in 1935 to be formed in Benedictinism, eventually returning to found St Gregory's Abbey. More recently a new flowering in the UK occurred in 1987 when the nuns of Burford opened their community to men, a development (now at Mucknall, Worcestershire) which subsequently gained an ecumenical dimension when a Methodist minister was solemnly professed.

> The monastic community has ... a special role – a prophetic role – in the present age: to be the Church as a contemplative community, and thus to bear witness to the primacy of the action of God in the affairs of mankind. (Gregory CSWG 1983, p. 4)

Monasticism reminds us that the heart of baptism concerns redirecting our *interior* life so we may love as Christ loves: 'for you have died, and your life is hidden with Christ in God' (Col. 3.3). It powerfully proclaims that, as we offer ourselves to others, we must be deepening our relationship with God – we need converting to God's reign. This is why the love of prayer and worship must precede everything else, as Jesus reminds us in commending Mary's choice while gently telling Martha: get your priorities right.

Unfortunately, rather than belonging to a mature university of life it can often feel as if we are living in a primary school where children fight for 'what's mine', more interested in little cliques and personal privileges than bigger questions. But as Fr Benson SSJE wrote:

> Your whole life must be a relative life. The moment you are imprisoned in your own self-consciousness, in your own separate individuality, in the selfishness of your own separate existence, you commit a worse suicide than taking the life of your body. You destroy the very life of your person ... Humanity is created to be a social being as God is a social Being. And as the three Divine Persons have no life whatsoever except in this relativity of action, so have we no life whatsoever except in relative action towards others ... It is the law of our nature that our life is personal, relative, communicating all that it has. It is the law under which the Christian church, the Body of Christ is constituted. 'They had all things in common.' Property belongs to the dead world. Community is the life of God. (Smith SSJE 1980, p. 36f.)

In a 2014 Retreat Address to his community, Fr Colin CSWG spoke of how the monastic tradition refers to its members as 'watchmen' who are to both guard this process and remain vigilant in making sure we abide in Christ. It is a role that is one of monasticism's great gifts to the Church, reminding us that we are constantly to be vigilant in this process.

Why, then, is this life often ignored? Has the Church forgotten that it points to the heart of Christianity? Are we uncomfortable with the radical way it asks us to prioritize prayer; that we aren't primarily called to function but faithfulness? It affirms, in particular, the centrality of a hidden life with Christ to enable the conversion of each member. Maybe a day will come when every parish church is a 'little school of the Lord's service', a place to which people look for guidance in prayer, meditation and service, where God can be found in silence. Until then, we need our monastics.

Monastic Vows

Happy are those whose way is blameless,
who walk in the law of the Lord.
Happy are those who keep his decrees,
who seek him with their whole heart.
(Psalm 119.1–2)

I always thought that Religious vows meant poverty, chastity and obedience. Then I discovered monastics take vows of obedience, stability and *conversatio (conversio) morum* (RB 58) – often translated as conversion of life. One Benedictine nun observed that, witnessing to the radical nature of the gospel, these vows focus into growth in the life of God. Just as Jesus wholly lived for and in God, so monastics seek to steep themselves in that life by growth in prayer, inner conversion and loving obedience, staying with it until death 'however hopeless it sometimes seems'. And because the Church can – and does – accommodate itself to the world, such a witness is vital.

Obedience

'Happy are those who keep his decrees, who seek him with their whole heart' (Ps. 119.2). The root of the word 'obedience' concerns attentive listening and monastic obedience requires giving profound, loving attention to the other rather than simply 'doing what you're told'. It was one of the vows I found hard – I want(ed) things done *my* way – but we're called to the way of Christ who was obedient to the Father (Phil. 2.5f.). Giving loving attention to the other prevents the 'self' from dominating and aids the path of humility to sanctity.

> They should each try to be the first to show respect to the other (Rom 12.10), supporting with the greatest patience one another's weaknesses of body or behaviour, and earnestly competing in obedience to one another ... To their fellow monks they show the pure love of brothers ... (RB 72)

It liberates from the dominance of self-centredness – 'this apple looks good – I'll have it!' (cf. Gen. 3). We must quietly listen with the ear of the *heart*, and that involves a certain internal detachment. In a culture revelling in the superficial, in-depth listening increases understanding and nurtures compassion as we learn to know ourselves and become aware of our powerful 'inner voices'. Maturity entails being able to discern the difference between those which are life-giving and those which are life-denying; those inviting us into deeper union with the Other, and those pandering to our ego-self. All that necessitates a certain stability so we can recognize what's happening in our inner 'cell'.

Stability

'My heart is firmly fixed, O God, my heart is fixed' (Ps. 57.7). This vow is a response to God's intimate love. Becoming aware of Love's call, we need (by the grace of the Holy Spirit) to be rooted in a desire to respond with heart and mind focused in Christ. Monastic stability involves commitment to a Rule and community which, with patience, enables that process whereby grace can work on nature in our deepening desire for God.

Of course, this vow is distinctly at odds with our instant, ever-changing, society. If we are constantly examining our roots or expecting quick results, growth will be problematic. This is why we need a Rule which includes contemplative practices (prayer and loving service) in order that the Divine within us might flourish.

Here are some other thoughts. Stability:

- and patience are good bedfellows; there are no quick fixes for encountering the depths.
- needs rooting in love.
- calls for a certain exclusiveness to guard our heart-cell where, like an expectant mother, we're pregnant with the divine: 'the kingdom of God is within you' (Luke 17.21).

- requires us to stay with something even when the going gets tough and we're tempted to seek distractions or look for another way.
- is about the whole of life, not just the religious bits. We aren't simply to be those who 'go to church', but people who are rooted in Christ 24/7.
- challenges the urge to travel aided by cheap holidays, mindless (not mindful) of the cost to the planet. How often do we ask ourselves – what's the point – will we see more than yet another swimming pool?

Together with obedience stability aids silence, stillness and awareness of God's deepening presence, holding us into that process of on-going conversion. Yet there's a paradox: for monastics affirm the truth that we are but strangers and pilgrims on earth. Let our stability, then, be in the Heart of Jesus.

Conversatio morum

> I treasure your word in my heart, so that I may not sin against you. (Ps. 119.11)

Rather than external change, monastic life affirms the importance of inner conversion. This vow is about the heart which needs to be re-formed through being re-fashioned, open to the creative Word and Spirit. Our heart needs purifying, not so we might feel 'better', but so we can live out the commandment to love with the whole of our being.

> Today if you hear his voice harden not your hearts. (Ps. 95.8)

Conversio reminds us that we need to make sure our 'salt' isn't tasteless (Matt. 5.13). That we need to cleanse our hearts by confessing our sins – 'Jesus Christ, Son of God; have mercy on me, a sinner' – reminding us of the value of the sacrament of Confession about which I wrote in *The Mystery of Faith*. Through honest confession our baptismal commitment is refreshed, and the light of Christ can again shine brightly in and through us. One Malling nun pointed out that such 'heart-change' will act like yeast and affect those with whom we are involved: 'for as the heart of an individual becomes more Christlike, so will the community of which we are part.'

PURIFICATION

He sits, the purifier
And refiner of silver,
Purging humanity's metal
By fire. I try to remain
Still under his hand,
To accept separation,
Removal of dross, whatever
Promotes inner and outer
Purification. Submission
Leads to clear perception
Of his beauty, though it take
A lifetime to reflect it.

Sister Honor Margaret CSMV

Contemplative Living

Enter into yourself, leave behind all noise and confusion.
God speaks to us in the great silence of the heart.
(St Augustine of Hippo)

The contemplation of God is the purpose of life (Rev. 22), so it shouldn't be surprising that many are drawn to this Life regardless of religious beliefs for, said Fr Gilbert Shaw (*Spiritual Warfare*, 1966), it brings the eternal Christ-life into

the here and now: 'Contemplatives must become as a city set
on a hill – to bear witness to the recovery of vision that the
whole church needs.'

> The contemplative soul is the instrument of Divine Love. Its
> contemplation is creative in so far as it is surrendered to the
> Divine Love. It operates not in its own self-expression but in
> and through the power of God: possessing nothing for itself
> and therefore possessing all things. (Shaw 1959, p. 73)

But some are unaware of this, forgetful of deeper needs. While
we can't all live in monasteries anyone can live more contemplatively even though certain aspects are divine gifts, and
some need this Life because of their primary call to prayer.
But, whatever our vocation: 'the life of the Christian is funda-
mentally mystical since it is the participation in the life of that
fellowship which is the mystical body of the Lord' (Benson
SSJE 2020, p. 27).

> There always have been – and there always will be – those
> whose compulsion is contemplation. Mary the Mother of
> God and Queen of contemplation, John the Divine to whose
> care the Lord committed her, Mary of Bethany who sat at
> His feet and heard His word, these are but the first of a long
> line of men and women who have had no other thought in
> life than the contemplation of God. (A Sister OSB, *Religious
> Life: Contemplative and Enclosed*, 1934, p. 2)

Having been drawn to places of prayer I sought the wisdom of
Religious whose discernment I grew to trust, monastics who
were living a more recollected life. Such a life involves repentance and living in the present moment, seeking to be aware of
God in all things.

Fr Gregory CSWG tells how William of Glasshampton
maintained that the

recovery of Religious Life in the Church of England cannot be seen as complete until the contemplative communities … have become firmly established, not only in respect to their own ideals, but (and here is still the challenge) in living relation to the church as a whole …
Our difficulty today is that we are so immersed in the temporal as to have lost sight of the spiritual, to have lost sight of God. (Gregory CSWG 1983, p. 3)

Contemplation doesn't just involve certain prayer practices. We mustn't be envious or greedy for spiritual perfection by finding 'better' methods, and need to be careful not to mistake practice with purpose; and the purpose of all prayer is union with Love by the hard road of dying to self.

We need contemplatives who are poor in spirit, yearning for God and the things of God. Those who give attention to the inner 'movements of the spirit', learning to discern which are from God and which lead into darkness; who remind us of the vital importance of paying attention to God in all things, pointing to the necessity of self-renunciation and simplicity while seeking to be lovingly centred on the goal of their desires and showing commitment to others.

Perhaps St Paul gave the best description of the primacy of this life when he wrote: 'If you have been raised with Christ, seek the things that are above, where Christ is, seated at the right hand of God. Set your minds on things that are above, not on things that are on earth, for you have died, and your life is hidden with Christ in God' (Col. 3.1–3). And because clergy have a vocation to aid others on their faith journey they need to nurture their contemplative heart.

If we are to have Jesus as our friend, we must know Him to be continually near. The companionship of Jesus! It is strange how many there are who look forward to being with Him in another world, but never think of living in fellowship with him here. (Fr Benson SSJE, ssje.org/2014/09/01/look-to-the-glory)

Mary, woman of prayer

> O Mary,
> pray for me
> that, listening,
> my heart may trust
> and be filled with the fruits
> of thanks and praise.

Looking back, I realize that, like Mary of Nazareth, it is when I've said my own 'fiat' (yes) to turning to God that life has ultimately flowed with a richness and sense of purpose. It is that 'yes' which allows the Spirit to be creative within the heart, moulding us to become what God is creating us to be, and enabling Christ to be formed. That doesn't mean everything's plain sailing. Like Mary, I've experienced periods of pain and deep confusion and have had to learn to be patient with God's workings – my 'yes' needs to be accompanied by 'Jesus, I trust in you'.

> MARY, Mother and Maid,
> Mary, perfect solitary,
> God's garden enclosed, keeping
> and pondering in thy heart,
> the secret of eternity.
> Mary, refuge of sinners,
> help of the weak, Mother of Mercy,
> pray for us. Help us to accept
> at every moment
> GOD only, nothing but GOD.

Sr Elsie Felicity OSC of Freeland gave me a hand-painted card bearing those words for my novicing. Sometimes I've been aware of the movements of God when my heart has been opened and I've been reassured and delighted by the experience, but often I've been confused and 'in the dark'.

I've learned that what matters is our patient practice of prayer regardless of our feelings. Religious look to Mary because she was the faithful one, God's handmaid, who allowed him to form in her womb. Her 'yes' inspires ours; her quiet, unassuming role a reminder of the importance of not pushing 'self'. Her life involved deep sorrow as well as joy, reminding us that God is present in both. Like her the 'quality' of our prayer can't be measured by how we feel; what matters is how we truly abandon ourselves, in faith, to God, trusting that by doing so God will work in and through us.

There have been times of great consolation when my faith and love have been deeply aroused, but the experience passes (although the memory is sustaining). Like Mary, I need to open my heart to God in longing love so that the Spirit, constantly present, may have room to flourish (Rev. 3.20).

Mary the humble one,
the still one,
offering a space in the
womb of her heart
for God:
her simple
'let it be'
bringing forth the Word.

Carmelites, Poor Clares and Others

For it is the God who said, 'Let light shine out of darkness',
who has shone in our hearts,
to give the light of the knowledge of the glory of God
in the face of Jesus Christ.
(2 Corinthians 4.6)

Over time, contemplative communities began to re-establish themselves. Inspired by Carmelites, Cistercians, Poor Clares,

Julian of Norwich and others they place great emphasis on solitude, silence and enclosure and what follows is a glimpse into some Orders and those who inspired them.

The Society of the Precious Blood (SPB), a name arising from the spiritual dedication of the month (July) in which they were founded, is a community whose Rule is based on that of St Augustine. Beginning by serving in the slums of Birmingham, UK, they eventually sensed the call to a more silent, prayerful life – from action to contemplation. Now, at Burnham Abbey, Buckinghamshire, the Eucharist flows into their daily 'watch' before the Blessed Sacrament where prayer for the world is offered.

I have always found places where the Blessed Sacrament is reserved to have a unique quality – whether the Sacrament Chapel in Alnmouth Friary overlooking the North Sea or the tabernacle in a parish church, the Eucharistic presence of Christ draws me into adoration and intercession. For those in need, the homeless refugee, the lonely person trapped in their room, the:

> ... first and greatest act of intercession is adoration of the Creator of all living creatures, who holds all souls in his hands ... the second is thanksgiving. Before we can ask, we must give thanks and praise, and bless God for all that he is in himself. Lastly, before we ask we must make a great act of submission to the Will of God, 'Not my will but thine be done' ... the perfect act of intercession as an act of love, of trust, of faith and of submission ... We may tell God what we want but not what he had better do about it ... (Mother Millicent in Felicity Mary SPB 1968, p. 78)

REAL PRESENCE

Just kneel
in the Real Presence.
Christ is there – transcending
tabernacle, aumbry, pyx –
the white light of immanent glory
proclaims. Always there:
saying 'I am Love,
so, love one another.'

Adore this Sacred Presence.

He is with you,
His wounded Body enfolds yours,
His sacred Blood
flows through the world's veins.

Tell him you love Him;
share the world's pain;
hear Him say –
'my Heart bleeds with love's wine'

I love you, too.

Yes, Jesus, you are blest,
praised and hallowed
in the Bread of Heaven.

The Community of the Servants of the Will of God (CSWG),
located deep in Sussex woodland, seek to nurture and offer
the fruit of William of Glasshampton's life of prayer. Their
semi-solitary life, based on Benedict's Rule, is also informed
by the teachings of their other co-founders, Frs Gilbert Shaw
and Robert CSWG. They also draw on the great tradition of
Orthodox spirituality, reminding us of its riches, not least its

emphasis on the work of the Holy Spirit, offering an expression of a wisdom we sorely need.

> Divine strength ... is displayed in incredible weakness in Christ. So we too follow that path of self-abasement and going down, and discover the humble Lord present in us. We each become a place where the Son ascends and returns to the Father. The sign that the powers of the human soul are functioning harmoniously is stillness and peace. This may happen only for a few moments, sometimes for longer, but at these times the soul is listening and receiving wisdom and knowledge ... This humility and self-giving unites us with Christ and his humble descent and we meet him in the lowest place. Here we learn more about him and about ourselves and, in dependence on him, work against those sinful tendencies which he exposes to us for our repentance ... This generates profound love and thanksgiving in the heart, and so it goes on. (Colin CSWG, Community Retreat, 2014)

For a while, some members lived in a deprived part of Hove, Sussex, and if you've ever sensed spiritual forces of darkness at work in the world, then contemplative life offers a powerful means of intercession in the heart of that conflict.

St Clare of Assisi (1194–1253), like her brother-in-Christ St Francis, wanted the gospel to form her. Recognizing the terrible dangers of wealth and pride she embraced absolute poverty. Finding God in simplicity, especially through creation, she invites us, now, to take time to be present to God's love.

Her life inspired a dispersed congregation in the Episcopal Church of the USA and the Community of St Clare (OSC) in Oxfordshire whose service is prayer. Everything else they do is intended to support and encourage them in that life and their work mostly uses only their hands or bodies, leaving their minds free. Coupled with that awareness of God-in-all-things, Clare shared with Francis a profound love for Christ in the Blessed Sacrament, and in her 'Third Letter to St Agnes of Prague' (another Poor Clare) wrote:

Place your mind before the mirror of eternity!
Place your soul in the brilliance of glory!
Place your heart in the figure of the divine substance!
And transform your whole being
into the image of the Godhead Itself through contemplation!

Julian of Norwich (c.1342–1416), author of *Revelations of Divine Love*, inspired the Order of Julian of Norwich (OJN) whose worldwide family, guided by Benedictine vows, are committed to prayer, intercession and conversion of life in the spirit of Julian.

St Teresa of Avila (1515–1582) was a Carmelite whose teaching informs and inspires communities in the UK and USA. In *The Interior Castle* she writes of the soul being like a diamond castle containing many rooms through which we need to pass. But the doorways are beset by 'poisonous reptiles' intent on preventing us approaching the centre where the fire of God's love blazes, a love that longs to set us alight. Her insights, like those concerning the 'dark night' by St John of the Cross, influence the spirituality of the Sisters of the Love of God (SLG).

[The sisters are] called to witness to Christ's repairing of human disobedience by the sanctification of its members through their union with the life of the incarnate Son of God. The Sisters shall therefore strive by their discipline, prayer and constant self-oblation to fill up what is behind of the afflictions of Christ *for his Body's sake*, using their privileges of enclosure and silence as a means to lead them in the power of the Holy Spirit to this union with God through Christ. (SLG, *Rule*)

That intention was developed by Fr Lucius Cary SSJE when, in 1943, he wrote to them:

the soul which has had some glimpse of Eternal Light, some sense of the Glory of the Divine Truth feels an irresistible attraction to set forth on the way of light, to seek by the Holy Spirit through prayer, discipline and reparation to gain more and more of that Divine Light that shines from Christ and in His Light and His Love to come at last to the unveiled vision of God ... It's in the hidden ways of God that every act done in faith does something to clear the soul's vision, to purify the eyes by which we are meant to see ... By faith the soul is chastened and strengthened and gains clarity of vision and increases in love.

There are others. The Society of the Sacred Cross (SSC) near Monmouth in Wales, for example, witnesses to a deeper life to be lived through the way of utter simplicity, loving faith and profound prayer. We need their wisdom, yet

Contemplatives in the world have a difficult time – because they are often isolated and sometimes not understood, particularly by priests. They need the support and encouragement of a place where contemplative prayer can really flourish. The object of a contemplative community is to be a home for contemplative prayer. (Shaw, *Recovery*, unpublished paper, 1961)

Malling Abbey

5

For the Sake of the Kingdom

Serving God Through Those in Need

'If you wish to be perfect, go, sell your possessions,
and give the money to the poor,
and you will have treasure in heaven;
then come, follow me.
(Matthew 19.21)

More than a century before St Teresa of Kolkata became
famous for her ministry among the poor, a dozen or so
Anglican women had begun similar pioneering work. Noticing
the plight of those living in the growing urban slums or in rural
poverty and the work done by Roman Catholic Orders, several influential people, including politicians, considered only
Religious could adequately address these problems (and also
provide a cheap solution).

The Catholic Revival in the Church of England and elsewhere had begun and some, realizing that the Religious Life
was present almost from the beginning of the Church, believed
it needed to be restored. At the same time, various (often
wealthy) women, fired by their faith, desired to embrace that
Life to reach out to those in need. Faith for them, far from
simply being a source of comfort, was the inspiration for heroism. Moved to minister in appalling conditions, without access
to modern medication and sometimes dying consequently, they
sought to care for the poor by providing decent nursing and
proper education. Instead of being condemned to sit idly in

the stifling comfort of their drawing rooms, often suffering the dictatorial behaviour of fathers and husbands, they found liberation through the Love that called to them.

Some of the great Anglo-Catholic churches nurtured communities of sisters who, within the context of a life of prayer, cared for the impoverished. From the start, many were subjected to vicious attacks as they worked in the slums, cared for the sick, set up schools and developed feeding stations (Rom. 8.37). Their embrace of the Catholic Revival brought about a charge of betraying Protestantism while showing indiscriminate care; no wonder they had to be strong-minded and clear-visioned. Unfortunately, the conditions many lived in during Victorian times are re-emerging and politicians still seem unable (or unwilling) to address them, leading some Religious to live in small groups in deprived areas that, with open doors, can be signs of the kingdom.

Despite Jesus' revolutionary statement that those who wished to follow him must 'hate' their families (Luke 14.26) the earlier Evangelical Revival had promoted them, stressing that home was the proper place for women. Sisters, therefore, were regarded as dangerous because they wouldn't conform; there were critical speeches in Parliament and many bishops at first refused to approve what they were doing. Rather than being unpaid housekeepers, they were serving the 'lower classes' thus threatening the social order. Refusing to have their lives ordered by men and actually voting for their superiors (who, themselves, were women) they were, indeed, revolutionary.

You came to serve God, and not please yourself.
Find your pleasure in doing his will, and beholding his glory.
(SSM, *Principles XXIX*)

A Call to Women

We are to be a means through which Christ lives on
earth in adoration of God our Creator, desiring that
the divine glory may be manifest, God's sovereign rule
come and purposes of love be accomplished. And also
we are to offer ourselves in love as Christ did for the
world's healing and reconciliation with God.

(CSC, Our Vocation)

Four years after Victoria became queen in 1837, Marian
Rebecca Hughes, believing God was calling her to become a
Religious and devote her life to the care of the disadvantaged,
was the first Anglican since the Reformation to live publicly
under the 'evangelical vows' of poverty, chastity and obedience.
She was just 24 and would later found the Society of the Holy
and Undivided Trinity which, along with others, sent sisters
to help Florence Nightingale nurse the wounded during the
Crimean War. The Society came to an end with the death of
the last sister in 2004.

Pioneers

In 1846, Anne Ayres, a member of the Episcopal Church of
the USA, felt a similar call and made vows before the Revd
William Muhlenberg in New York, subsequently developing
the Sisterhood of the Holy Communion.

Mary Jones, the 'dearest friend' of Florence Nightingale,
became Mother Superior of the Nursing Sisters of St John the
Divine (NSSJD – now the Community of St John the Divine
(SSJD), immortalized by the British television series, *Call the
Midwife*. Harriet Brownlow Byron founded the Society of All
Saints Sisters of the Poor (SASSP) in 1851, setting up the first
UK School of Nursing at University College Hospital, London,
followed by one in India. Thirteen years later, Etheldreda
Benett joined their novitiate in preparation for founding the
Sisters of Bethany (SSB) in the Clerkenwell slums. She then

established a large orphanage near Bournemouth and concern for women's spirituality led her to organize the first retreat for them in 1866, prior to which such a thing was considered unnecessary.

> I alone can decide
> between giving whole-heartedly of myself
> and my energies,
> or limiting my giving.
> (ASSP, *Rule*, 1980)

Harriet Monsell began the Community of St John the Baptist (CSJB) at Clewer, near Windsor, in 1852 and rapidly developed many important social projects. Long before Josephine Butler began her celebrated campaign, these sisters were working among prostitutes and other marginalized and excluded women, establishing a community in New York in 1874.

Two years later Teresa Newcomen founded an Order in north-east England that became known as the Community of the Holy Rood (CHR) among whose members Sister Dora, the 'Florence Nightingale of the Midlands', is the most famous.

In 1870 Emily Ayckbowm started the Community of the Sisters of the Church (CSC). She had become aware of the plight of the street children described by Charles Dickens in *Oliver Twist*. Little was being done for them by way of education and she wanted to nurture their spirits as well as their minds. Eventually she established about 30 schools in the UK and overseas under the care of her growing community. Concerned with children's health, she also founded orphanages and convalescent homes where they could be cared for, the largest of which were in London and Broadstairs where, eventually, over 800 children could be accommodated.

The plight of the navvies building the Metropolitan Railway through Kilburn also came to her attention and she set up canteens for them, then for London dockers and others striking for better working conditions. She was also severely criticized for aiding the 'undeserving poor' to whom she showed 'indiscriminate charity', as documents of the time reveal, but this was all part of that 'Church Extension' work in which she passionately believed.

Typical of other sisterhoods, the first members of the Community of the Holy Name (CHN) shared in the terrible poverty around them but weren't simply religious social workers. 'It was out of a burning love for Jesus and desire to glorify him', said one of the sisters,

> that our Foundress placed all her teaching about mission work; it was useless for her to minister in her own strength, she could only go with Jesus, and without him she could do nothing. His love had to overflow from her heart to all the world. (Dunstan 2015, p. 81)

In Canada, Hannah Grier Coome founded the Sisterhood of St John the Divine (SSJD) in 1884 after serving a novitiate with the Community of St Mary (CSM) in Peekskill, New York. During the First World War Margaret Cope founded the Order of the Holy Paraclete (OHP) in Whitby. They follow the Benedictine tradition, and became an important teaching Order with large-scale work in Ghana and Southern Africa. Mother Margaret was instrumental in fostering relations between the Church of England and Church of Sweden, helping to develop Religious Life there.

These and many others, moved by compassion, realized faith demanded action and, placing their trust in Christ, bravely and fearlessly attracted many to a consecrated life of service. Most were drawn to a 'mixed' life of prayer and action which, in the words of Mother Emily CSC, 'most nearly resembles the life of Jesus on earth':

> Always remember that it is you, your faithfulness and loyalty, your personal holiness the Community values and not the work you do – although that is valued according as it is the expression of your Religious Life and not just work done … It is not what we do, but how we do it that matters … The habit of doing common things with uncommon care

is what will make us saints ... (Mother Emily's Message, 5 June 1900)

The nursing Orders filled the space left by the 'Sairey Gamp' type, critically written about by Charles Dickens in *Martin Chuzzlewit*; this played a vital role in the advancement of professional nurse training and led to senior nurses being called 'Sister'.

Worldwide developments

Mother Etheldreda SSB agreed to the Archbishop of Canterbury's request in 1890 to send sisters to help the Syrian Orthodox church in Kurdistan. Unlike other missionaries they didn't want to convert people to their denomination but worked alongside the local churches, something which reflected her deep desire for Christian unity as well as helping promote good relations with the Orthodox.

There is nothing in the world except the glory of God. (Mother Etheldreda SSB)

As Orders grew, bishops around the world began inviting them to make foundations, often resulting in the development of indigenous communities. Of their foundation in Lesotho, Mother Agnes SPB wrote: 'Our community started with the poor and for the poor and to begin again with Christ's poor in such poverty and obscurity draws us strongly' (Felicity Mary SPB 1968, p. 158).

Consecrated to the love and service of God's reign, they went where they were called. They weren't perfect; their need to be strong sometimes led to some being regarded as stubborn and, like us, they reflected aspects of their society many might now question. Yet still their work can be pioneering. In 1982, 120 years after the All Saints Sisters of the Poor developed professional nursing, and seeking to follow their foundress's teaching to be 'relevant to the present day', they opened Helen

House, the world's first hospice for children, and four years later founded 'The Porch' to serve the Oxford homeless.

Call of the gospel

It was the gospel that inspired them to do great things, something shown by the example of the Community of St Mary the Virgin (CSMV). In 1884, the new priest of the quiet Oxfordshire market-town of Wantage saw the appalling physical and spiritual conditions in which the rural poor lived and decided to do something. Like others he had been raised an evangelical and moulded by the ongoing Catholic Revival and not only wanted to address the deprivation of the town, but to restore the sacramental life of the parish, a dual mission offering an important example today. Theirs is still a 'mixed' community whose commitment to the Divine Office and Eucharist is matched by social action, echoing a famous speech by Bishop Frank Weston to the Anglo-Catholic Congress of 1923:

> If you are Christians then your Jesus is one and the same: Jesus on the Throne of his glory, Jesus in the Blessed Sacrament, Jesus received into your hearts in Communion, Jesus with you mystically as you pray, and Jesus enthroned in the hearts and bodies of his brothers and sisters up and down this country. And it is folly – it is madness – to suppose that you can worship Jesus in the Sacraments and Jesus on the Throne of glory, when you are sweating him in the souls and bodies of his children. It cannot be done. (*Our Present Duty*, http://anglicanhistory.org/weston/weston2.html)

The Community's ministry eventually included running a leading drug and alcohol rehabilitation centre, refuges for women and work with prostitutes. Like others they found inspiration through Mary who stood by her son: from Bethlehem to Calvary, the Sorrowful Mother accompanied the God few recognized. The first sisters found their hearts 'magnified' – enlightened and encouraged – as they offered themselves to

God, and '*fiat mihi secundum verbum tuum*' ('let it be to me according to your word', Luke 1.38) became their motto.

Later, a young woman, Agnes Mason, was inspired to create the Community of the Holy Family (CHF) to help Christian teachers and artists consecrate their calling to Christ. She had been sitting in an olive tree in Florence when she suddenly recalled Shakespeare's words in *The Merchant of Venice*: 'Who chooses me must give and hazard all he hath' (Act 2, Scene 7), words which were the seeds of what became an international Order. Their Rule stated that: 'It is greatly desired that the Community of the Holy Family may become a home of real learning and art by receiving and by educating student and artist Sisters.'

While the last sister died in 2010 their charism has inspired a new dispersed teaching order in the USA composed of those prepared to go and help change the lives of those who have been 'written off'.

A Call to Men

The Catholic religion is one of sacrifice,
of good works done for love of Jesus.
(Raynes CR 1959, p. 148)

'Un-manly, un-English and un-natural' was one response to the idea that men might want to live together and take vows of celibacy (Best 1967, pp. 117–25). The first stable Anglican religious community for them since the Reformation, the Society of St John the Evangelist, had been established in 1866 by Fathers Richard Meux Benson, Charles Grafton and Simeon Wilberforce O'Neill. Known as the Cowley Fathers from the part of Oxford where they began, they quickly expanded to North America, India, South Africa and Japan and had a profound effect on the development of both the Religious and spiritual life of Anglicans.

As the Industrial Revolution drove more people into the cities and poverty grew, communities continued to develop and a number were informed by the principles of Anglo-Catholic socialism, all of which, no doubt, was a matter of great concern to some Englishmen.

Christian socialism

The development of socialism had a considerable effect on the Catholic movement. Many of the first Religious, drawn to minister amongst the deprived, realised how it expressed aspects of the gospel and related to their own vow of poverty. As eligibility for voting expanded, the moral character, vision, and pastoral heart of the person a Religious elected was understood to be important – as well as reflecting something of the nature of the electors.

Charles Hopkins was 23 when, in 1884, he started championing the rights of seafarers and helped develop the precursor to the National Union of Seamen, going on to develop the Society of St Paul (now the Order of St Benedict, Alton Abbey) as a response to their needs. That same year Fr James O. S. Huntingdon founded the Order of the Holy Cross (OHC) in New York to enable social justice through prayer and active work.

The Community of the Resurrection (CR) at Mirfield, Yorkshire went further and had a definite connection with the development of late nineteenth-century socialism. Avoiding attempts to have an abbot, they sought to integrate a degree of individual liberty within the concept of corporate authority and many of their members, not least Fr Trevor Huddleston CR, were prominent in the South African anti-apartheid movement.

Most of the first brothers of the Society of Divine Compassion (SDC), founded in 1894, were profoundly informed by similar principles although believing: 'Socialism must be Christianised or it would shake Christianity to its foundation, precisely because it appeals to the higher and not the lower instincts of man' (Beer 1919, pp. 176–8). In 1914 they, together with a small community of sisters, began the first residential work in England for those suffering from leprosy, based at East Hanningfield in Essex. Never having many members, the Society came to an end in 1952 and the Society of St Francis (SSF) took on their work in Plaistow while the leprosy work was continued by the Sisters of Bethany until the 1980s.

The first and best gift we can give to the world in which we live and work is the gift of praying personalities. We must be true to our stewardship, ever seeking to raise and never to lower the standard of our life of prayer. We need to bring our spiritual consciousness to our Lord that we may learn to think as He does. When we reach out hands that are consecrated by wounds, we shall really be able to bear one another's burdens. (Andrew SDC, Wednesday after Sexagesima, 1934)

Today there are many men's communities in the Anglican Communion, the largest of which is the Melanesian Brotherhood in the Pacific Islands.

Homelessness and the marginalized

Like many, my twenties were a decade when I wanted to make a difference. Shocked to discover young people living on the streets of London I volunteered at Centrepoint, a homeless shelter in Soho where I met brothers of the Society of St Francis, one of whose founders, Br Douglas SSF, had a long history of caring for the homeless and unemployed, often joining them on the road.

In 1922 Douglas had been asked to take responsibility for the Brotherhood of St Francis of Assisi (BSFA) at Flowers Farm, Dorset (now Hilfield Friary) which consisted of a fledgeling community of brothers and wayfarers. He went on to inaugurate hostels throughout the country and helped establish the Vagrancy Reform Society which provided important information to the government leading to major improvements in Casual Wards and the passing of the Public Assistance (Casual

Poor) Order in 1930. After World War Two he was asked to minister to troops in war-ravaged Europe where his compassion for those suffering in refugee and prisoner of war camps led to him being named the 'Apostle of the Outcast'.

In India, Father Algy Robertson had joined the Christa Seva Sangha (CSS), an Anglo-Indian ashram (spiritual monastery) founded as an attempt to enculturate Christianity, which generated the Brotherhood of the Love of Christ in England. Eventually he and Douglas joined forces to create the Society of St Francis.

The Poor Man of Assisi

The three Orders founded by Francis are now present in the Anglican Communion: an 'active' First Order of men (and, now, women – the Community of St Francis, CSF), a Second Order of contemplative Poor Clares (OSC) and a Third Order (TSSF) for men and women 'in the world'.

With that profound understanding of God's presence in all things and his celebration of the masculine and feminine hidden in creation, Francis sought to overcome dualism and enable people to realize their divine splendour. His spirituality offers a balance between the redemptive – all things in need of restoration, and the incarnational – God present in matter, which he realized was most fully revealed in the Blessed Sacrament:

> Behold, each day he humbles Himself as when he came from the royal throne into the Virgin's womb; each day He himself comes down to us, appearing humbly; each day He comes down from the bosom of the Father upon the altar in the hands of the priest. As he revealed himself to the holy apostles in true flesh, so He reveals himself to us now in sacred bread. (*Francis of Assisi* 1999, vol. 1, p. 129)

We must thank Franciscans for maintaining the truth of our inter-relatedness: we're *all* brothers and sisters no matter our ethnicity or station in life. Francis resisted the lure of rank, title or educational achievement and, conscious of being a sinner, was deeply moved by Christ's Passion which led to his receiving the marks of the Crucified (stigmata). This didn't overwhelm him because his heart was fixed on the utter loving mercy of God, and he rejoiced in an ever-deepening relationship with Jesus which involved having a complete commitment to 'Lady Poverty', something we'll look at in the next chapter.

> The friar's integrity is the same as that of everyman. It is to stand before God and say 'Yes'. (Bernard SSF, in Samuel SSF et al. 2008, p. vii)

Forgotten treasure

Today, the Church can seem oblivious to the groundbreaking witness of these Orders. Their life has a spiritual richness, yet the Religious vocation, even though reflecting the essence of life in Christ, is often ignored.

> All Christians are called to holiness; we as a religious community are called to be a visible witness to this truth, to God's absolute claim upon all life. Whatever else we do or accomplish, if we fail to respond to this call to holiness, we are like salt that has lost its taste. Faced by so great a calling, aware of our own weakness, we need not lose heart. God will use all that we are and everything in us, for it is God, the source of holiness, who will make us holy. (CSC, Introduction, *Rule*)

Every founder/ress expected much of themselves and those who joined them, and their compassion attracted others. Religious I have known who have exerted a powerful influence have done so because they were the 'friends of Jesus' and offered that friendship. Nurtured by their catholic faith, evangelical joy and rooted in a deep listening to God at work in the world, active ('mixed') communities are also committed to a life of prayer. The founder of the Society of Saint Margaret (SSM) said that Jesus present in the Blessed Sacrament was the 'central light' of the sisters' devotion (Anson 1955, p. 345) while others deepen that relationship by offering the Rosary and many are still engaged in aspects of whatever charism lies at the heart of their foundation.

It could be argued that Religious Life was God's greatest gift to the Anglican Communion as people responded to Jesus' call to embrace poverty, seek chastity and offer obedience for the sake of the gospel. Neither the thought of their own comfort nor the desire for marriage and families was as important as that call. When Religious communities re-emerged there was no Anglican tradition on which to build; instead, many turned to what they could glean from continental Orders, finding inspiration through the spirituality of people like SS Francis de Sales, Jane Frances de Chantal and Vincent de Paul, each noted for their work among the poor. As they grew in faith and service they became 'giants in the earth' (Anson 1955, p. 83) and still challenge us – how am I serving Jesus?

And Still Christ Calls

Those heady days may have passed and some Orders, which did so much to address crucial social concerns and help create today's caring society, are now a shadow of their former selves. As the State has taken over their work and the Church they served becomes forgetful, still the Suffering Servant (Isa. 52.13f.) calls. These words, probably known by many early founders and foundresses, are as relevant now as then:

> We should not judge the poor by their clothes and outward appearance nor from their mental capacity. On the contrary if you consider the poor in the light of faith then you will see that they take the place of God the Son who chose to be poor. Although in his passion he almost lost the appearance of a man and was considered a fool by the Gentiles and a stumbling block by the Jews ... Since God loves the poor,

he also loves the lovers of the poor. (St Vincent de Paul in Atwell 2016, p. 546)

We suffer with Christ as we seek to live the gospel life and embrace the Divine will rather than our own, taking up his cross: thy kingdom come, thy will be done on earth as it is in heaven. In whatever way it's expressed, Religious Life is for the sake of the kingdom, reminding us of the importance of our baptismal vows.

The spirituality that animates each Order not only provides its lifeblood but also informs its ministry and touches those it encounters. The desire for God needs to be the dynamic behind *any* ministry, something the medieval English mystic, Walter Hilton, wrote about in his book, *The Mixed Life*, in which he talked of the way, through good works, prayer and spiritual reading, we must fan the flames of the love of God to prevent the fire of that love dying out.

Those flames have fired evangelistic work at home and abroad. For many years I, along with others, took part in missions to parishes, prisons, schools and universities as well as leading retreats and teaching weeks. Part of the importance of Religious Life is that it can speak to many who might not otherwise be attracted by the churches, yet all of us are to work for the Reign of Christ. We might join with others concerned with matters of justice and peace, open our eyes to his presence in movements towards human liberation, consciously realize ourselves as Jesus's brothers and sisters in our place of employment, and see him in those amongst whom we live. The Holy Spirit gives gifts to each of us to cherish and nurture for the benefit of the Kingdom: what's the spirituality that animates your faith?

We are created to be social beings, as God is a social Being. And as the Three Divine Persons have no life whatsoever except in this relativity of action, so have we no life whatsoever except in relative actions towards others. (Benson SSJE, MS. viii, 156)

6

Vowed for Life

Poverty, Chastity and Obedience

The Vows are a threefold response of love,
given to us in love that we may love.
The vows open us daily to the mystery of the cross:
they set before us the beauty of the pearl of great price;
they challenge and beckon, support and direct us,
that we may be brought, with all God's people,
to the vision of his glory.
(CHN, *Rule of Life*)

'Repent', according to Matthew (4.17), was the first word
Jesus spoke as he began his public ministry. It's challenging
and hardly attractive, yet helps give substance to our faith
and resonated in the hearts of the Desert Elders. Repent! Turn
around! Begin again!

Repentance, in the Church of England's rite of Baptism, is
expressed as the rejection of the 'devil and all rebellion against
God, the deceit and corruption of evil and the sins that separate
us from God and neighbour' and that rejection lies at the heart
of the Religious vocation. Monastics vow obedience to their
abbot/abbess and, stable in their cell, seek the conversion of
their lives to Christ. But by the twelfth century, fundamental
social changes caused Francis of Assisi to understand the
world as his cloister. Jesus' response to a rich young man provided what became known as 'counsels of perfection' (Matt.
19.16f.), those fresh expressions of what it means to be wholly

consecrated to Christ through 'evangelical vows' (counsels) of poverty, chastity and obedience which Fr Benson SSJE said in a sermon he preached at the Jubilee of St Barnabas, Pimlico in 1900, offered a 'highway to God' providing a 'shelter of the Spirit.'

'If you wish to be perfect, go, sell your possessions,
and give the money to the poor,
and you will have treasure in heaven;
then come, follow me.'
(Matt. 19.21)

They are 'evangelical' because their purpose is to enable the likeness of Christ who was poor, chaste and obedient and, if embraced with loving generosity, enable fullness of life. Reflecting the baptismal rejection of 'the world, the flesh and the devil', those 'three great enemies of the spiritual life' (SSF *Principles*, Day 4), they were adopted by many of the early, non-monastic Orders. In 1965 the Community of the Transfiguration offered this description of the vows in their Rule:

First, to be a sign of Christ in his detachment from all to belong to all – a sign of Christ's poverty by which he made all rich, a sign of Christ's chastity that he might become the Brother of all and the Father of the poor, a sign of Christ's obedience that he might give to everyone his true freedom.

Evelyn Underhill, the important early twentieth-century spiritual guide, wrote in *The Mystery of Sacrifice* (p. 25f.) of the way that offering our 'natural' life to God enables the 'supernatural'. Reflecting the way these vows have always been understood to focus our response to Christ and enable prayer to have a priority, she saw their embrace as the means of offering the loving gift of self as an oblation, a living sacrifice. And, in words which the Church might consider in our own time, she wrote that the vowed life 'again and again sums up and discloses the true nature of her deep interior life: the poverty of spirit, the chastity of heart, the obedience of will, which are the marks of an entire self-abandonment, and therefore the condition of her supernatural power.'

The way of Christ

The vows offer the *way*; keeping them is not the end, and anyone seeking to live by them needs to be wary of perfectionism: humility must be their guide. Many, now, are cautious of vows, so the notion of Life/Perpetual Vows can seem odd – pointless. Yet to be committed to the lifelong way of Christ involves the pilgrim committing to an ongoing and ever-deepening relationship with God, although a time may come when a Religious needs releasing from them.

> What is it to be consecrated to Jesus Christ, if we are not absorbed in His love. (Benson SSJE 2020, p. 156)

They are informed by the Incarnation – the enfleshment of God in Jesus the Christ (meaning 'anointed one') – for such a spirituality involves a certain poverty where one holds nothing back; a chastity of life given to the love of God, and obedience to God's call. All that helps enable the revelation of the mystery of God uniting the earthly and heavenly, practical and contemplative, bodily and spiritual contained in an inner cauldron of love: love of each for the other fired by the divine flame (cf. 2 Cor. 5.14).

> May the power of your love, Lord Christ,
> fiery and sweet as honey,
> so absorb our hearts
> as to withdraw them from all that is under heaven.
> Grant that we may be ready
> to die for love of your love,
> as you died for love of our love.
> (St Francis of Assisi, *The Absorbeat*)

This cross of Love has both horizontal and vertical aspects, as Fr Gilbert Shaw pointed out in talks to the Sisters of the Love of God. As we take up our cross the eye of our heart needs to be fixed on the life coming to us from God *and* from the world of human relationships. It's not an easy intersection because we can feel worldly pressures telling us to give up or give in to pleasing the self. We will struggle and our failings will constantly come to the surface, but we need to be trustful and faithful and leave the fruit-bearing to the Holy Spirit. What matters is our commitment to prayer and the offering of our lives while leaving the rest to God.

Poverty

Do not love the world or the things in the world.
(1 John 2.15)

During the Sermon on the Mount, which began with the Beatitudes, Jesus says: 'where your treasure is, there your heart will be also' (Matt. 6.21). Those words resonated in my heart, why does 'stuff' have such an appeal? Material possessions can imprison and blind us to our need for God, while the embrace of Religious poverty frees the heart to be filled by God.

This vow points to the ultimate absurdity of 'possessions' because, at some point, they'll all have to go: house, belongings – people – and where then is our treasure? I try to remember that everything is lent for a season by God who will ask me to account for my response to them: 'where your treasure is ...' Just as the vow is a response to the way that 'the love of money is a root of all kinds of evil' (1 Tim. 6.10) so it affirms that our dependency needs to be rooted in God – which might be hard but is what all Religious founders believed, enabling them to realize a depth of joy in possessing nothing: 'Jesus, (can) I trust you ...' But trust can be hard, especially if people have let you down.

Poverty also concerns that freedom whereby I don't seek to possess things or people. I need to develop a loving detachment whereby everything is received as gift for which my heart needs to be thankful. To let go of feelings of annoyance when there are things I cannot do because I don't have the means, and of envy at what others have. I need to use my gifts, no matter how seemingly insignificant (as Fr Benson taught), for the glory of God.

Blessed are the poor

Although Benedict believed his monks should be provided with basics, Francis of Assisi adopted a more radical approach to the 'goods' of this world. Recognizing how dangerous possessions can be, he rejected personal and corporate ownership and 'wed' Lady Poverty. He wanted nothing to be labelled 'mine', standing in the tradition of Jesus saying in Luke's gospel: 'Blessed are you who are *poor*, for yours is the kingdom of God' (6.20). Matthew, however, seems to have influenced Benedict: 'Blessed are the *poor in spirit* ...' (5.3) which isn't the same as being spiritually poor; it's having the humility to know your need of God and resist that little devil – the master of lies and deceit – who whispers in your ear: you deserve *more*; *you* can do it.

Both opposed the notion of profit-driven economics, believing goods should be shared for the benefit (well-being/good) of everyone. This reflects the life of the Trinity whose Being is about mutual sharing, reminding us that life isn't about maximizing what we can get, but what we can *give* for the good of all. A Church without those who have embraced this truth is in danger of forgetting the gospel of Christ who taught that through the way of poverty we come into a right relationship with God. 'In all things', say the *Principles* of the Society of St Francis, 'let the brothers and sisters exhibit the simplicity of true Franciscans who, caring little for the world where they are but strangers and pilgrims, have their hearts set on that spiritual home where their treasure lies' (Day 7). So, we hitchhiked whenever possible, wore donated clothes stored in the 'Jolly Cupboard' and sought, in a phrase probably coined by a former Episcopalian, St Elizabeth Ann Seton, to 'live simply [and joyously – *pace* St Elizabeth], so that others may simply live.'

Heavenly treasure

The account of Jesus' meeting with that rich young man (Luke 18.18f.) really hit me when I was 26 because, like him, I was seeking something and Jesus' final response to the question 'what must I do to inherit eternal life?' resonated: 'sell all that you own and distribute the money to the poor, and you will have treasure in heaven; then come, follow me.'

I'd heard them many times, but on one occasion they spoke into my heart – if you would be *perfect* go, sell, give … This was the royal road sought by the Elders and all who have heard the call into a deepening relationship with God – they realized it involves what we do with our credit cards as much as our prayer books. Now I am no longer a First Order brother I still ask myself – where does my treasure lie? It can be hard, in a culture identifying us as consumers, to resist that 'I have, therefore I am' feeling.

> The more poor and empty, the fewer little treasures the Religious has, so much the more she is the bride of the Blessed Sacrament and of him who is poor. The more she gives up so much the more she can say … 'O God, Thou art my God.' (Mother Frances Mary CHN in Dunstan (ed.) 2015, p. 80)

Every loving sacrifice is a step on the way of holiness. Jesus warns us of the dangers of acquisitiveness and the importance of an uncluttered heart for God to fill; of the way we're to be stripped of whatever prevents growth: 'Every branch that bears fruit he prunes to make it bear more fruit' (John 15.2).

Penury and justice

But biblical, and therefore Religious, poverty isn't penury, that
extreme lack of resources making life impossible. The biblical
'poor' (Hebrew: *anawim*) are the lowly who enter a new, liberating relationship with God expressed through dependence,
obedience and praise:

> The joy of the poor in spirit does not lie in having nothing,
> but in finding everything in God.

(CSC, *Rule*)

Religious often grapple with this, recognizing that justice
demands joining the struggle to overcome that involuntary,
barren poverty which causes profound damage, reminding the
Church that it must always make, as Fr Pedro Arrupe SJ said
in a letter to the Jesuits in 1968, a 'preferential option for the
poor'. Many are involved in various movements for justice,
peace and the integrity of creation (JPIC) and all Franciscans
belong to a UN organization that advocates for the protection
of human dignity and environmental justice.

Letting go

Then there's that matter of poverty which comes through
tragedy. I've heard people who've suffered misfortune speak
of 'friends' gloating over their loss; once gone, the wealth that
attracted others proved like dust in the wind.

How natural it seems to lament what we lose. Once, while
hitchhiking, I became anxious and irritated on discovering
I'd left something of importance in the car in which I'd just
received a lift. With no way to contact the anonymous driver,
I began to fret until one of my brothers said – 'Just give it
to God!' And, with a struggle, I did and discovered freedom
through that detachment.

The common tendency to accumulate things and become hoarders even of trivialities needs to be resisted, as also the temptation to spread personal belongings around the house, invading common areas and others' limited space. A turn out once a year could be a good exercise! (CSC, *Rule*)

But possessiveness isn't just about material things. Mother Jane SLG used to remind her sisters that they might find it harder to be detached from plans and opinions than from material things. No wonder St Francis, on a long journey with Br Leo, once insisted he consider where perfect joy can be found: not from hungering and thirsting for wealth, fame or success, but freedom from the demanding 'self'.

Cooperation, competition and community

We need to remember that at the heart of our faith lies a Trinity of Persons – Father, Son and Holy Spirit: Christianity is rooted in Divine cooperation. I wonder what this belief in a communal, Three-in-One God who exists in perfect equality might say to corrupting competitiveness and a 'winner-takes-all' mentality?

The beauty of the Trinity can easily be masked by the ugliness of greed revealed in the pollution of both planet and people. Witnessing to the importance of cooperation, Religious Life affirms that wealth is about realizing, as Julian of Norwich saw in the simplicity of a hazelnut, that the whole world is there for our delight and isn't something we can ever 'own'. The good things we have are for the glory of God.

Yet even though the vow of poverty isn't about promoting the notion that having nothing is good, some of the most joyful people I've encountered were the – mostly Christian – garbage collectors of Cairo. Living in large communities among the rubbish tips on the outskirts of the city they were filled with an inner radiance animated by their commitment to Jesus, his Mother and the saints, something which shamed this Western pilgrim.

The commonality of Religious Life also means that much is shared, not least cars. What lifestyle changes might we make to reduce pollution? Imagine how much cleaner the air and less competitively aggressive we might be if, whenever possible, we abandoned private vehicles in favour of public transport.

Saved through poverty

The vow asks, where are true riches to be found? Consider the generosity of God: how generous can I be? To what am I enslaved? The way of greed, arrogance, pride, jealousy and envy is cursed; how can I set my heart on God and his kingdom? The fact that this is the first of the three Evangelical Vows indicates its importance and we need to consider the challenge it poses to the way we live.

From the time of the Elders possessions have been recognized as dangerous; yet penury is wrong, greed a sin, and our insatiable appetites morally – and mortally – dangerous. In 1888 Fr Benson SSJE said to the Manchester Church Congress: 'We need Religious in the present day, *not so much to save the poor from their poverty, as the wealthy from their wealth*' (italics mine). Those words are as true now as then; the vow, however it's expressed, reminds us not to let 'things' distract our heart from being set on the way of Christ; rather, to live simply, freely, generously and joyfully for the sake of God's reign.

Holy Lady Poverty,
may the riches I find in you
    be my consolation,
and the freedom you give
    be my joy.
Make my heart firm in its embrace of you,
and nourish your seed in my life.

Chastity

Chastity of mind is fed by truth.
Chastity of heart is deepened in prayer
and fostered by love which casts out fear.
It is weakened by dissipation of mind and heart,
by idle curiosity and gossip, murmuring, disloyalty,
jealousy, ill humour, and insensitivity.
(CSC, *Rule*)

People don't often talk about the virtue of chastity, yet to live a chaste life can be a beautiful thing; it means desiring to live through the great commandment to love God with heart, soul, mind and strength; and neighbour as self.

Chastity isn't about being sexless but requires us to harness those energies, which can become disordered, in creative and not dissipated ways. It helps us attend to what the heart is set upon and guards us from desiring to have what is not ours. It is intimately connected with Jesus' saying, 'Blessed are the pure in heart, for they shall see God.' According to the Rule of the Sisters of the Love of God: 'It is in chastity, which is the whole being set on God, that the hidden joy, which is beyond all natural attainment, will be found.'

It concerns more than abstinence. Embracing our whole being, it involves – by God's grace – a cleansing of our passions rather than their suppression, keeping the heart free of whatever might lead it astray. 'Lust', wrote a sister, 'is but one of the passions. We also need to purify our greed, anger, impatience, selfishness, possessiveness and the other emotions that interfere with relationships. Purified passions are still there within us, but they do not dissipate or exhaust our energy' (Stebbing CR 2015, p. 101).

Celibacy, chastity and sexual abstinence involve for us a direct offering to God of our whole person, our capacity and need for love, our sexuality, and creative energies, all of which are the Creator's gifts to us. Since we are created in God's image the more we grow to understand and value our humanity, the more we shall enter into a divine mystery and into the life and love of our celibate vocation. (CSC, *Rule*,)

Anyone can make a vow of chaste celibacy but members of the Single Consecrated Life (SCL) do so publicly in the context of everyday life, something which is to be discerned with your spiritual director and priest.

Being loved

Some time after joining the Franciscans I began to wonder if, as a child, I had been really loved. Healing came when I realized my parents had loved me in the way they could, which wasn't, necessarily, the way I wanted. All of us need to *know* we are loved, and this vow cannot be an escape from love (which is its humus); so if, as an adult, we become aware that we lacked love in childhood then, by God's grace (and the help of a good spiritual director) we will need to face that lack and seek Godly healing.

This vow also requires an abandonment to Love. Such abandonment can purify and nurture that love we are called to live out: the love we have for the Beloved teaches us how to love with a more perfect love those we are given to love, whether we are called to celibacy or not. 'Set your minds on things that are above, not on things that are on the earth', wrote St Paul (Col. 3.2–3), 'for you have died, and your life is hidden with Christ in God'. At one time, when making Life Vows, women Religious were considered 'brides of Christ' and, for a while, I tried to develop an understanding of being 'married' to Christ (marriage has never simply concerned people of opposite sexes). But it's a struggle to keep attention on 'the things above' and we'll need to repent when we give way to temptations.

Celibacy

Many are single not by choice but for other reasons and, probably, never considered this call. But if they've lived as a single person for long, they might consider embracing celibacy. Religious have done so and are aided in this decision by the way Jesus remained unmarried for the sake of the reign of God. He alluded to celibacy when he declared: 'For there are eunuchs who have been so from birth, and there are eunuchs who have been made eunuchs by others, and there are eunuchs who have made themselves eunuchs for the sake of the kingdom of heaven' (Matt. 19.12). Eunuchs are men who, to perform a particular service, have been castrated and those who demand that someone live as a celibate should remember that it's a costly vocation 'possible only if we are anchored in God in faith, in hope, in prayer; responsive to the work of the Spirit within us. Otherwise, celibate life is sterile' (CSC, *Rule*).

> Most Holy Lady Chastity,
> may my deepest desire for you
>   be strengthened in Christ;
> may your beauty be my delight
> and your grace my comfort.
> Affirm your presence in my life.

While the vow gives freedom from certain family responsibilities it doesn't preclude establishing bonds of friendship which, in a community, can be intimate but not exclusive. The very notion of being a 'brother' or a 'sister', says one Rule, means that members are called into familial, intimate relationships not least because it's through such relationships we can be mirrored. We need others to help us see both our dark and light sides and I learned to be grateful to those brothers who loved me non-judgementally, who saw and encouraged the best in me while helping me turn from the worst and, by their loving concern, helped me want to change.

Having said that, as a gay man I am fortunate that my faith wasn't formed through churches whose teachings about homosexuality have, by their simplistic interpretation of certain scriptures, caused terrible damage. Thankfully, Religious Life helped me to accept and celebrate my sexuality.

We pray Thee, Rising Light serene,
E'en as Thyself our hearts make clean; ...
Our roving eye from sin set free,
Our body from impurity.
(*English Hymnal*, 55)

The sexual celibate

Still, there's a loneliness about celibacy, for the need for intimacy is hard-wired in us: 'it is not good that the man should be alone' (Gen. 2.18). Genital urges, that driver that helps maintain the species, are means of connectivity. Our sexual energy can propel us in many ways but can be focused through creative relationships harnessed by the reins of love. However, while most find fulfilment through sharing life with another, some need to embrace this call rather than just being single as a way of enabling their loving.

We all need to come to terms with the need for physical intimacy. Everyone makes mistakes and we can find forgiveness and the grace to continue through the sacrament of Reconciliation, a sacrament to which I've often returned in my struggle to be fully human. Celibacy isn't easy, at least I didn't find it so and, for anyone with a high sexual drive or wanting children, it can be very difficult to avoid becoming sexually involved with another, not least when our sexual drives awaken and need to find a means of expression.

At times many of us will miss having fathered children. We shall need to open the poignancy of this loss to Christ in prayer. He will show us that in union with him our lives have been far from barren. As we nurture others in Christ, and bring them to maturity, we shall discover that fatherhood has found expression in our lives. In prayer, meditation, our thought, our work and our friendships, we are called to fulfil our deep human urge to be creators with God of new life, and to bear fruit that lasts. (SSJE, *The Rule*, p. 20)

Hard work might re-channel some energy but there are times when it's only by the grace of God acting on our will that we can avoid inappropriate intimacy. Growing in the grace of chaste celibacy won't be helped if attention is, for example, given to pornography which feeds lust, one of those sins called 'deadly' because of its poisonous effects. Rather than toying with feelings (or seeking to suppress them), being profoundly thankful can reduce their intensity and prevent them controlling us. But whether single or celibate we need to know how to direct our passions so that they serve rather than rule us. As Abba Gerontius of Petra (*c*. fifth century) observed:

> Many are they who, tempted by the delights of the flesh, indulge in sexual immorality in the mind without any physical contact. While preserving their physical virginity, they revel in mental sexual immorality. Beloved, it is good to do what is written, 'Keep your heart with all vigilance, for from it flow the springs of life': Prov. 4.23.

One of the arguments of the Reformation was that the Bible doesn't require celibacy of priests, leading some, when Religious Life returned, to condemn the vow. Anglicans have always regarded celibacy as a gift, knowing the importance (not necessity) of genital intimacy for human flourishing, and it's clear that to deny someone not called to celibacy the possibility of sexual expression can force them to drive it underground where it can wreak havoc, and those churches which try to 'convert' LGBTI people might need to repent of the damage they are doing. Unlike Jesus, churches can seem more interested in matters of sex than wealth and poverty.

I've known some wonderful Religious who, owning their sexuality, are alive with its wonder, but that's usually the fruit of struggle. It's a life that looks to Jesus' chaste intimacy with the Father and often connected with nurturing deep and close spiritual friendships, such as Jesus had with St John the Beloved, to 'let the mystery of God penetrate us', as Fr Gilbert Shaw once observed.

Our vow flows also from the experience of Christ ascended and glorified dwelling in our own hearts. Though we have surrendered the fulfilment we may have found in marriage or partnership, the mystery of union and mutual love is truly given to us. In the emptiness and absence that celibacy opens up in our hearts, Christ waits to make known to us the infinite strength and tenderness of his love. The exploration of our sexual solitude through prayer will reveal the depth of Christ's desire to be the one joy of our hearts. We can find the joy of celibacy only by entering into the mystery of our union with him and returning his love. (SSJE, *The Rule*, p. 19)

Obedience

Those who love me will keep my word,
and my Father will love them,
and we will come to them,
and make our home with them.
(John 14.23)

'Do what you're told, or I'll speak to your father!' is a threat I still recall from childhood. But Religious 'obedience' is less about doing what you're told, and more about listening carefully to the Other. For the word comes from the Latin *audire*, to hear.

Autocrats demand tyrannical obedience which, once given, can result in dehumanization. Abusive acts can occur when someone gains power over another, and despotic leaders can render people childish. But learning forms of obedience to beneficial norms can enable creative disciplines. Through obedience to my piano teachers, I learned to play reasonably well – and it's important to obey the Highway Code. Following certain disciplines makes daily life both possible and easier and, in a similar way, obedience to a spiritual Rule can help develop our life in Christ, just as obedience to the law of love enables us to grow in him (Rom. 13.8–10).

> Our obedience is expressed, not merely in acts, but in a style of life, an attitude which regards life in terms of service rather than rights, one of self-emptying love and humble serving, such as we see in Christ's washing of the disciples' feet. (CSC, *Rule*)

Reflecting Christ's obedience to his Father: 'I have come down from heaven, not to do my own will, but the will of him who sent me' (John 6.38) it's the vow common to all Religious. By addressing Adam's rebellion (Rom. 5.19) it undermines the lure of self-centredness and enables community but must never become the excuse for wrongdoing or cause anyone 'on any authority [to] act contrary to the guiding of their own consciences' (SSF, *Principles*, Day 11).

Listening

Once we get away from understanding obedience as the blind following of orders and consider it as in-depth listening, we can begin to understand its relevance to matters of faith. Mary's response to God as she listened: 'Here am I, the servant of the Lord; let it be with me according to your word' (Luke 1.38), reveals a truer understanding of the vow. This directs us back to her transformative 'heart-listening' as she attended to the 'Word' who is God.

I vividly recall being blessed in many ways when I sought to really listen to what was being asked of me in community especially when, sometimes, my initial reaction had been to say 'no'. As a young novice I was asked to preach Holy Week at a large private boys' school, a request that caused me to panic – I felt utterly inadequate and *knew* God didn't want me to work with teenagers! The thought of giving daily talks at Chapel (compulsory), run groups and 'be around' filled me with dread. But as I listened, I managed to say 'yes' and that simple *fiat* ('let it be ...') eventually led to 20 creative years of ministry among young people.

The second, quite different, request to which I first said 'no' was to become an assistant prison chaplain. That wasn't my calling either! I had no experience with such places and was fearful of criminals: 'They'll just make fun of me ...' But, in the end, with trust (but no enthusiasm) I again said 'yes' and when, eventually, I left I did so with tears in my eyes knowing how much I'd received from ministering among often profoundly damaged, locked-away men.

Each request seemed bizarre and frightening but as I listened – both to my Guardian (community head) and to the movement of the Spirit – I realized the importance of being obedient to what I was hearing, and that made all the difference.

Discernment

Obedience is clearly connected to the process of individual and corporate discernment as we try to listen to God through a multitude of voices:

> The paradox of choice means that sometimes the more freedom we have, sometimes the more trapped we can feel. Have you ever stood in the grocery store, confronted with one-hundred options for a can of tomato sauce, and wondered what was the point of it all? This is the paradox of choice: too much freedom can leave you feeling powerless and unable to move forward in a worthwhile direction. The monastic way has always embraced limitation as life-giving. Sometimes less is more. Living within the limits set by our community, in obedience to those in authority, has the incredible ability to set us free. (SSJE, catchthelife.org)

Just as obedience requires attentive listening, so discernment helps us make good choices where these are possible. We need to have sufficient freedom so we can respond with those three great theological virtues of faith, hope and charity which bring a greater sense of consolation as we seek to attend to living in Christ. Discernment involves being aware of those interior movements, those 'good and evil spirits', and seeking whatever will be for God's greater glory, a process needing to be shared with our spiritual director.

Leadership

While Benedictines owe obedience to their abbot and Rule, Francis of Assisi wanted all to be brothers (and sisters) in Christ, served by ministers, because he understood the dangers of being a 'leader' (a 'Magister/Master'). It was Br Damian SSF who showed me that anyone responsible for others needs to exercise authority through humble, joyful, generous service. Informed by the compassion of Christ, Damian always led by example leading many to listen and respond to him. A good minister is one who is not subject to the ravages of changing moods but reveals a humble stability in the Heart of Christ.

Humble obedience

Obedience is what husbands and wives/partners sometimes vow and all need to practise – to listen to the other as they would to Christ – and I wonder what's lost if the vow is omitted? It isn't a matter of subservience or an abrogation of responsibility, but a means of defeating self-will and pride while valuing and honouring the other. This call to renounce the 'fallen' self applies to every Christian; all are called to nurture that self which bears the image and likeness of God until 'it is no longer I who live, but it is Christ who lives in me' (Gal. 2.20).

In rushing to become masters of our own destiny we can become enslaved by our primitive instincts and impulses. But in seeking to renounce self-will and live in obedience to Christ and his reign, the Religious offers yeast to the Church. For if we forget the power of the unseen forces of evil which constantly appeal to our lower nature, it's easy to see what can happen.

> Obedience in all its aspects should be accepted faithfully as a means of uniting oneself with the will of God. Humble work under obedience thereby fosters prayer. There need therefore be no tension between the time in the community Rule designated for work and that set aside for prayer. Altogether the aim of the Vow of Obedience is to ensure the unique peace of Christ within the common life and the hearts of the members of the community, a peace that can enfold those who come to the community for rest and retreat, and flow out for the benefit of those who live in the surrounding area. (Gregory CSWG 2008, p. 23f.)

Whether Religious or not, we all live in some form of obedience and our response can aid or hinder our growth in humility, the servant of this vow. Looking back to moments when my rampant ego has been challenged, I realize how obedience to an-other can gradually undermine those twins of self-will and pride. To become Christlike, full of grace, means reflecting his perfect obedience to the Father.

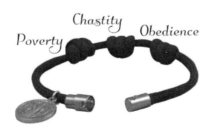

Poverty *Chastity* *Obedience*

Let the same mind be in you that was in Christ Jesus,
who, though he was in the form of God,
did not regard equality with God as something to be exploited,
but emptied himself, taking the form of a slave,
being born in human likeness.
And being found in human form, he humbled himself
and became obedient to the point of death –
even death on a cross.
Therefore God also highly exalted him
and gave him the name that is above every name,
so that at the name of Jesus every knee should bend,
in heaven and on earth and under the earth,
and every tongue should confess that Jesus Christ is Lord,
to the glory of God the Father.
(Phil. 2.5–11)

7

Habits and Hearts

Clothed in Christ

Let your priests be clothed with righteousness:
let your faithful people sing with joy.
(Psalm 132.9)

The brown habit I placed over my head each day, cut in the shape of the cross, was a reminder to 'put on the Lord Jesus  Christ and make no provision for the flesh to gratify its desires' (Rom. 13.14). This is a high calling, and over the years I've encountered many Religious whose lives reflect the habit they wear; Religious like Father Aelred Stubbs CR whose quiet, unassuming life contributed greatly to the anti-apartheid movement in South Africa. Some lived in communities, others as solitaries, but all were part of that great river flowing from the heart of Christ, a river he invites us to drink from and which is to flow through us (John 4.1–15).

Baptismal life

Baptism is the means whereby we're made one with Christ, yet is regarded by many as a one-off event rather than affirming a desire to share in the living, dying and rising of Christ affirmed through every Eucharist. We are made one with his offering, his life enfolding ours so that God might be revealed in and through us as we seek to live with compassionate love and fragile faith. 'Our witness to Christ's love in us is a growth in the loving obedience of faith and the laying aside of our self-centred love' (Shaw 2018).

United with the love of God-in-Christ we must learn the humility of dying daily to sin. It's not always easy to reject evil and turn (again and again) to Christ, to abandon our lives to him and seek to live out his reign, but that's what life in the Risen Christ concerns (Luke 9.23f.).

> One of the fruits of desiring this union is a deep sense of joy which is there even in times of darkness and difficulty, giving cheerful courage in the face of disappointment, and an inward serenity and confidence through sickness and suffering. (Third Order SSF, *Principles*, Day 29)

Vocation to union with God

Baptism concerns our response to the God who is searching us out, desiring that the wonder of divinity shine through us. Like a sculptor, God seeks to fashion us into unique beings conceived within the divine Heart. That's why we sense that incompleteness, that feeling there's something needing to be realized. For God calls us to awaken to the promise of who we can become (yet, hidden in God, already are). Religious Life, primarily, concerns reconciliation with that Being whose desire for us is all-good and all-loving. We need to refine the ear of our heart to hear God's call and not turn from it; to keep our eyes fixed on Christ lest we sink beneath the waves (Matt. 14.30).

Putting on 'the Lord Jesus Christ' is symbolized by being dressed in a baptismal garment with words such as: 'You have been clothed with Christ, as many as are baptized into Christ have put on Christ.' In Religious Life this is mirrored by 'clothing' a novice with the habit of their community:

Receive the habit of this Community of St Mary the Virgin, a sign of the putting on of the Lord Jesus Christ, and be clothed with humility; in the name of the Father, and of the Son, and of the Holy Spirit. Amen. (CSMV, *Clothing of a Novice*)

It is then that another work begins. According to the fifth-century Elder, Diodochos of Photike, after the Spirit of God has replaced the spirit of evil in baptism, evil then attacks seeking to plunge its 'tentacles' into us as it tries to regain its place. Thus, we become involved in a combat to enable the Holy Spirit to completely possess our heart so that, finally, she comes to shine out through us (Bouyer 1961, p. 206).

Personal dedication

Just as we are named at our baptism, so many Religious take on a new name when entering community. This can be done at Confirmation or Ordination and some also make a personal dedication to an aspect of our faith. For example, realizing that devotion to the Incarnation, the Mother of God, the Blessed Sacrament and so on enables a deepening of their faith, they become known in their communities as Br X 'of the Cross' or Sr Y 'of Jesus'.

Because it's a personal dedication it could be useful for anyone if it helps increase faith and love. So, for example, you might dedicate yourself to the Divine Compassion of Jesus (and/or Mary) and then pray that you might live out of that dedication. You don't need to tell anyone, although it would be helpful to talk about this with your spiritual director.

Clothed in Christ

... he has clothed me with the garments of salvation,
he has covered me with the robe of righteousness,
as a bridegroom decks himself with a garland,
and as a bride adorns herself with her jewels.
(Isaiah 61.10)

If you were asked to picture a Religious, you might conjure up
the image of someone dressed in a habit. I still recall looking
down from the top deck of a bus when I was about six and,
seeing a group of women entirely clothed in black, asking my
nonconformist mother who they were. 'Nuns,' she replied in a
slightly disapproving voice. Many years later when first wearing
my habit in public, it was with a sense of embarrassment mingled
with pride as I wondered what people were thinking of *me*.

As I put on the long habit with its wide sleeves, I tried to
recall St Paul's words: 'May I never boast of anything except
the cross of our Lord Jesus Christ, by which the world has been
crucified to me, and I to the world' (Gal. 6.14). The hooded
cowl placed over my head was a reminder of how Christ had
said, 'Take my yoke upon you, and learn from me' (Matt.
11.29), and the white rope bound me to him: 'I have been
crucified with Christ ...' (Gal. 2.19), made clear by the crucifix
some wear. Others may be given a golden ring at Life/Solemn/
Perpetual Vows to symbolize their marriage to Christ.

The way we dress can show who we are – or what we represent: the bride in her wedding dress, the nurse in their uniform,
the priest in black. Yet the habit is more, for it speaks of him
whom Religious seek to reveal. Often, I struggled with what
those garments represented compared with what I knew about
myself, for while the proverb 'clothes make the man' might be
true, I was also conscious of the fact that 'the habit doesn't
make the nun'.

In his book, *History of a Religious Idea*, Fr Herbert Kelly SSM
said that the habit was a witness for the benefit of others, but
most of us can't display our faith in such a way. Some Christians
wear a cross and Coptic Orthodox normally have one tattooed

on their wrists, but even that doesn't quite express this matter of being clothed in Christ, unless you wear a devotional scapular.

What we wear and who we are

A sister once talked with me about feeling closer to Muslim than Christian women for she, like them, was modestly covered by a long dress with a veil making her realize her 'indwelling' in God. Another told me of visiting an exhibition concerning the symbolism of the veil, especially in Islam, and suddenly seeing how she was enfolded in God 'from head to toe'. Each morning, when the sisters of another community place the veil over their heads, they offer a prayer which affirms they are covered in 'God's wings'.

In Western culture the notion of modesty seems to have taken a back-seat: 'I alone ought to decide what it's right to wear and if that's shocking, that's not my problem.' Yet what we wear can express something of our inner world and we need to consider whether an element of humility is needed. Humility, so central to life yet so counter-cultural, not only reminds us that attention needs to be given to the other more than self, but that it is the antidote to the ego running riot. All things might be lawful, but are all things beneficial (1 Cor. 6.12)? Our clothes may have greater symbolic value than we admit or realize.

> May Christ and his Saints
> stand between me and harm.
> Mary and her Son.
> Patrick with his staff.
> Martin with his mantle.
> Brigid with her veil.
> Michael with his shield.
> And God over all
> with his strong right hand.
> (Celtic prayer on dressing)

COMING OUT

Yes, look at me, and see:
this is who I am,
and this is the love that has found me.

The truth was insistent, but I kept it secret,
hiding in shadowed corners from curious eyes,
flinching from questioning,
fearing pitying looks,
dragging my feet, held back
by family hurt and bewildered, sensing betrayal
(what? no grandchildren? ever?),
and a church that smiles on the normal,
calls this selfish, not knowing how to believe
there could be another way
for love to warm the world -
and, stronger than these, my own small, grudging heart,
not yet ready to risk
what such a love might claim.

But that's all over now.
There'll be no more disguise;
it's time to put on the gear.
The ankle-brushing skirt
and the hair-concealing veil,
the unapologetic crucifix,
the knots for binding vows,
the unambiguous 22-carat ring –
let them all shout aloud in the world's incredulous face,
'Look! look! my beloved is mine
and I am his.'

A Sister SLG

Might we benefit from beginning to give expression to the way God is present in everything – our morning shower a reminder of baptism, the food we eat the Bread of Life, the people we encounter hidden saints of God, the bed on which we sleep the grave in which we will lie. 'Whatever you do, in word or deed, do everything in the name of the Lord Jesus, giving thanks to God the Father through him' (Col. 3.17).

Recollected living

Yet as I settled into Religious Life such devotional understandings seemed aspects of antiquated piety. I read that Benedict wanted his monks to care for their working tools as if they were vessels of the altar and it seemed so out of date – we've got throw-away plastic now – surely our attention needs to be given to more important matters! Today I realize – what dangerously dualistic thinking.

For centuries everyday things were understood to have a devotional value. They helped nurture a recollected life where everything is done with care because the whole of life is meant to glorify God. Having discarded such hidden wisdom it's re-emerging in 'mindfulness practices', the fact that this was part of our spiritual tradition largely forgotten. But as we reclaim an understanding of 'recollected living', we come to realize that *everything* we do needs our loving attention: God is in all things.

Vocation

So, what do my clothes reveal? How might Christ view the way I adorn my body? I've struggled with questions like these – shouldn't my appearance reflect the beauty of Christ? After all I've 'put him on' and am to abide in him who abides in me (John 15.9). That indwelling, celebrated in every Eucharist, affirms that I'm part of the Body I consume. I – we – are to become what we feed on, and so I'm called to cooperate with the grace – the energies – God provides through that Sacrament if I *really* want to reveal myself as part of his Body.

Consequent to my baptism I began to realize that my life needed to change – I needed to find an outlet for those Christ-energies flowing through me (although I wouldn't have expressed it like that) so that my whole life might express what I affirmed:

Take my life and let it be,
consecrated, Lord, to Thee.

A new name

I had thought this concerned priesthood, but it was to be through Religious Life that I made a fresh start – was 'born again'. I was journeying like Abram who became Abraham and took a new name: I wanted a 'new man' to emerge in me. But it's one thing to change a name or wear the right clothes and quite another to have your heart set in the right place. Beneath any outer forms what really matters is – a heart aflame with God's love.

Turn the gaze of my heart to you, O God.

A New Heart

Take my yoke upon you, and learn from me;
for I am gentle and humble in heart,
and you will find rest for your souls.
(Matthew 11.29)

The Reformation may have obliterated monastic teaching about 'purity of heart', but when Lydia Sellon founded her sisterhood she was attracted by the Sacred Heart of Jesus and divided her Order into three branches, the second of which – enclosed at Ascot Priory – was known by that dedication. For whatever reason it was soon changed to the 'Love of Jesus' but a few years later Mother Teresa, Founder of the Community of the Holy Rood, proposed a devotion to the Sacred Heart (Manton 1977, p. 151), and the Society of Divine Compassion was dedicated to it (and our Lady). By 1914, William of Glasshampton wrote that vocation in the context of Religious Life is a personal call into the Sacred Heart of Jesus (Curtis CR 1977, p. 40) and many have found inspiration through this devotion.

Augustine of Hippo, whose Rule and spirituality informed many Anglican founders, is often depicted holding a flaming heart symbolizing the way, at his conversion, his own burst into flame with the love of God. 'You have pierced our hearts,' he wrote, 'with the arrow of your love, and our minds were pierced with the arrows of your words' (*Confessions*, 9, 2).

> LORD, I was made for Thee,
> So let me rest
> Not otherwise than on Thy breast.
> Let the pure thought of Thee
> Quiet my mind,
> In Thy dear Heart my heart
> Its haven find
> Yet, let myself, this little soul,
> Come to so great a goal.
> For though of clay Thou madest me,
> My clay was touched with Thine eternity,
> And I am 'restless till I rest in Thee'.
> (Andrew SDC, 'An Echo of St Augustine')

Before the Community of the Transfiguration emerged, Fr Roland Walls realized something was forming in his heart and shared with an Orthodox acquaintance his sense that living the gospel needs to be done through community. He was advised to make a pilgrimage to Patmos in Greece and talk with a certain monk and when eventually they were able to meet, Roland was simply told: 'Saint John was near enough to his Lord to hear his heart-beat'. This was what he needed to hear.

There is a long spiritual tradition focused on the heart, but some find the art used to depict Jesus' sacred, blood-red heart,  pierced by a lance, encircled by thorns, and crowned with the cross, rather off-putting. Perhaps this indicates that we've forgotten how images of the heart appeal to ordinary people; from those displayed on Valentine's cards to representations made by fingers and hands, the heart speaks of love. Yet the image of the Sacred Heart takes us further, for it shows the cost of love – the commitment, passion and suffering involved in keeping ablaze Love's flame.

> The cross is the attraction of the Religious Life ... and we have deliberately taken up a cross which is far too heavy, so of course we shall fall, again and again to the end of life. That doesn't matter, so long as we get up and struggle on with Jesus, never giving up, however many times we may fall, always taking up the cross again and again – carrying it after Jesus, with Him, for Him. (Curtis CR, 1977, p. 40)

> Sacred Heart,
> Burning in darkness,
> Enflame my heart

Focus on the centre of your being, symbolized by the fleshly organ pumping blood, where thoughts, emotions and will are united by the indwelling Holy Spirit. Here is the abode of the soul – that Godly aspect which can never be taken away, where we hear the Divine voice and encounter our-self if we 'listen carefully ... with the ear of (our) hearts' (*Rule of Benedict*, Prologue 1). Jesus calls us into this place of relationship with the Father: 'I came that they may have life' (John 10.10b). People have long been drawn to Jesus' heart and over the past thousand years, many Religious have written of how ours can be changed as we rest on his. That is an aspect of what is known as 'affective prayer' where the emphasis is the heart's desiring to love and devotion to the pierced and bleeding Heart can prevent a Christian understanding of love being too superficial. Religious Life might proclaim the primacy of God, but it can take a long time to realize just what that entails. Just because I wore that brown habit didn't mean I was completely abandoned to God. The conversion of my heart – my *metanoia* – was (and is) ongoing and difficult, as Mother Millicent SPB observed: 'God instructs the heart by contradictions, not by ideas' (Felicity Mary SPB 1968, p. 132). God is to be found both *in* my heart and beyond it, for the heart needs to be broken open if it is to be home to the infinity of God, large enough that it can be the stable where Christ is born, the doorway to eternity.

Man was made for God, and nothing less than God can satisfy him. Adam sinned because he failed in contemplation: ever after the heart of man was divided. Christ came, whose life was one ceaseless act of contemplation of the Father, His Heart, His Sacred Heart, raised always heaven-high. Not only in the wilderness, but at every moment of His earthly life he met the temptation to deflect his gaze to anything lower than the Father. (A Sister OSB, Malling Abbey)

Conversion through community

My Franciscan years taught me that this need for a changed heart is never an easy process, and I found it to be unlike any instant 'make-over'; rather than spending money on exercises to make the body beautiful, the cost involves wanting to be renewed in the Heart of Christ. Religious Life reveals that the heart is of far greater importance than external appearances.

In a reflection on 'spiritual conflict', Father Gregory CSWG reminds us that it is out of our heart that evil thoughts emerge (Mark 7.21–23) which need purifying through repentance, prayer and good works. If not, my heart will be subject to the forces of the 'world' of which I'll become the child.

A pure heart create for me, O God,
put a steadfast spirit within me.
(Ps. 51.10)

As I began to prayerfully attend to my heart within a context
of silence and solitude, I realized that God wanted me to be
cleansed of what had become buried; Christ opened my heart
to his reign as the Spirit worked for my enlightenment in the
context of community. I noticed memories and desires emerging, and the feelings associated with them were sometimes so
powerful that I needed a physical outlet – the odd mug thrown
from my window into the garden led me to understand that I
needed help to make sense of what I was experiencing. This
cleansing and renewing process uncovered memories which
needed to be processed with my spiritual director and, for a
time, a therapist.

> In this whole-hearted identification with Jesus in his Passion
> there is something which contributes to the great work
> of Divine Love revealed in the Sacred Heart of Jesus; it
> penetrates through the depths of the Divine Purpose; pro-
> motes God's mighty plan for the conversion of sinners and
> the salvation of the world his Son died to save; makes some
> real contribution to the sanctification of the Body of Christ.
> That something is a radiant self-communicating vitality of
> holiness. (Raynes CR 1959, p. 124)

Repentance

We've moved a long way from expecting prayer to be full of
light and happiness, but this note of interior contentment – 'it
satisfies' – offers a sure sign we are on the right path, a path to
be followed each day along which there's a constant need for
repentance.

By listening to our Lord and looking upon Him as He is
shown to us in the holy gospels we can penetrate into the

hidden depths of his Heart, be taken into that Heart and there rest in perfect peace and safety. (Benson SSJE, source unknown)

How I wish we gave more attention to the Sacred Heart! To rediscovering that his reveals what ours might be like: 'The Lord is gracious and full of compassion, slow to anger and of great kindness' (Ps. 145.8). Can I be merciful, compassionate, and kind? If that's the nature of the Sacred Heart, and if we are created in the image and likeness of God, then doesn't this identify what human-being is all about? About opening the heart until it becomes Godlike, large enough to enfold all. Each day, wonder and rejoice at God's hidden presence, not least in those who need compassion. After all, that's what inspired those pioneering founders.

We sense that God is worshipful and, indeed, we are sanctified by his presence and his touch as we dwell in him. But what Jesus has shown of the Divine nature is true of the numinous Being of the Father; he is above all compassionate, deeply caring, tender as a Mother, and ready to heal, restore, forgive. (Damian SSF, letter to the author)

In a talk to Religious, Mother Mary Clare SLG once spoke of how we are called to live at the point of intersection where the Love of God and the tensions and sufferings we experience meet. Unless we give attention to this 'intersection' within the heart an essential part of who we are will remain stunted and we will never, as the Elders expressed it, find the ladder leading to heaven. It wasn't just to monastics that Christ said: 'whenever you pray, go into your room and shut the door and pray to your Father who is in secret; and your Father who sees in secret will reward you' (Matt. 6.6), it was to everyone.

Heartfulness

Some who have become estranged from the Faith value 'mindfulness' practices, but the contemplative way of '*heart*fulness' offers the ability to be lovingly present to the Other, and not reactive or overwhelmed by what's going on around or within us.

Mindfulness practices can improve mental well-being by paying attention to the present moment, to thoughts and feelings, reflecting Christian teaching concerning 'recollection'. But post-Reformation Christianity became trapped by notions of 'onward and upward' rather than 'retreat and descend' and we lost touch with ancient practices encouraging us to befriend the caverns of the heart.

> In so far as we make ourselves ready to receive the gift of contemplative prayer, we shall be enabled by the power of the Holy Spirit to know for ourselves the realities of which the scriptures and the saints have spoken. (Fr Gilbert Shaw in Hacking 1988, p. 108)

The stillness of a Religious house can allow us to enter our inner 'cell', but external silence isn't as important as nurturing a quiet heart. Many say they don't have time for meditation, but you can enter that cell whenever you want. On the bus, walking the dog, sitting idly for a while and withdrawing your attention from what's going on around you, all provide occasions when we can nurture this place, and thus enable stability.

As people awaken to the importance of their inner world, we need to rediscover the treasury of contemplation, perhaps one of the most important 'fresh expressions' of faith needed today. St Paul recognized this when he prayed that 'with the eyes of your heart enlightened [may you] know what is the hope to which [God] has called you' (Eph. 1.18). The Elders practised what we now call Centring Prayer – that gentle repetition of a phrase in the heart – and for the Community of the Holy Name the sanctity of that Name is such that prayerfully breathing it into the depths of heart ('Je-sus') brings deep joy.

As the nineteenth-century Russian monk, St Theophan the Recluse, said: 'To pray is to descend with the mind into the heart before God and to go on standing unceasingly, day and night, until the end of life' (Ware 1997, p. 1) That reflects the older teaching of hermits such as St Isaac the Syrian that if we gaze deep within our heart, we shall find there the ladder that leads to heaven.

Penetrate my heart by the radiance of your glance

And when God begins to act directly in the heart 'all that is not of God', one sister said, 'is pushed up to the surface of consciousness' there to be blown away by the breath of love.

The whole place of the community becomes identified with the chapel sanctuary, and the whole life is offered as a sacrifice of thanks and praise. Likewise the cell, as the place of solitary prayer, becomes identified with the 'heart', which is supremely the place of the Spirit. Finally, heavenly and earthly sanctuary, cell and heart, all become one: the place of the Spirit, the place of the Epiphany of Christ, the throne of the Trinity. (Gregory CSWG, *Community Report* 1978, p. 14)

8

Priests and Prophets

Eucharistic Living

My heart is fixed, O God, my heart is fixed,
I will sing and make melody.
Awake my soul, awake lute and harp,
for I will awaken the morning.
(Psalm 57.7–8)

'I think I'll look for just one more job before I retire,' said
the priest. Such a comment suggests the priesthood is simply
another occupation; but is it a 'job' to be undertaken or a
calling from which you can never retire – that defines your
identity? And because baptism makes us part of Christ's royal
priesthood (1 Peter 2.9), this chapter should contain something
for everyone.

Priesthood, along with the diaconate and episcopacy, is
one of the Holy Orders of Ministry. Differing from Religious
Orders in that the vows normally associated with that Life
are not taken, they do share certain aspects, not least living to
the glory of God. At a time when it can feel as if the Church
functions according to secular models it is important to recall
that every priest is, primarily, a sacrament of Christ. They are
called to cultivate that relationship in order to declare the mys-
teries of faith, nurture his Body on earth with the sacraments
of grace and, caring for his members, reach out to all with that
nurturing Love that declares freedom.

The time I spent as a student at Kelham Theological College, then Mother House of the Society of the Sacred Mission, introduced me to the radical nineteenth-century educational methods of its founder, Fr Herbert Kelly SSM (1860–1950). He believed priestly training needed to be rooted in a life of prayer and sacrifice, community, fraternity and duty all informed by humility. He stressed that priests were primarily ordained to serve *God*, reflected by the Society's motto, *Ad gloriam Dei in eius voluntate* (To the glory of God in the doing of his will). That meant being grounded in the Incarnation, illustrated by a story told about Fr Kelly by Roland Walls, a former seminarian and one-time novice of the Society. He recalled (*Mole Under the Fence*, p. 175) how Father Kelly would take new students to the monastery's pigsty and ask them to look at one of the sows and, after five minutes silence, say: 'Now, God has either everything to do with that old sow or he's got nothing to do with anything in this world. You may go.' And that was the first lesson he taught to this group of 'sacristy rats'.

It was at Kelham I first experienced gathering around the altar during the Eucharistic Prayer, realizing that priest and people share in the work of liturgy. None were passive attenders but all were active participants, making sense of the fact that we said 'Our' and not 'My' Father and didn't sit in our personal space as someone said: 'Let us pray'. It wasn't easy to accept that God wanted me to 'stand in his presence and serve (him)', but I began to realize that the Eucharist isn't a private devotion but the occasion when the Body of Christ affirms itself. It offers that Body and is nourished by that Body to be that Body in the world. Worship, not galloped through as if there was a train to catch, was not only about giving glory to God but allowing God's glory to transform us.

Formed by Religious Life

The experience of being trained in the context of a community rooted in worship, informed by vows, and shaped by a common life has been extremely important for hundreds of priests. We learned the value of a regular life with daily rhythms of silence and prayer, study, relaxation and communal eating, something that would benefit anyone.

Four times every day a hundred students and brothers entered the great brick-built basilica-like chapel, crowned by a vast concrete dome blackened with the smoke of candles and incense. 'You can be toiling over your essay,' observed one 'and then a bell will ring, summoning you to prayer, and you have no choice but to go and hand it over to God!' Each morning I would gaze up into the darkness from which heaven would be revealed as we celebrated the liturgy. 'The great space behind the altar,' wrote another, 'seemed to set it at the edge of the world beyond which was the vastness of God's infinity. It was a house on the rim of eternity.'

Priests are ministers of Christ's Mystical Body whose buildings are places where earth opens to heaven. At Kelham I discovered the importance of celebrating the Office and Eucharist with the dignity, devotion and prayerful attention they deserve, because what is done in choir and sanctuary needs to draw heart and mind to God.

(Whoever) cannot keep silence is not contented with God.
(SSM, *Principles*)

Training, focused on glorifying God, was undertaken in a context where times and seasons of the Christian year, coupled with our interaction in daily life, enabled the formation process. We cleaned and polished, gardened, kept silence, played football (annually with the local Borstal) and cricket, making sure our learning was rooted in life. This, someone remarked, 'made priests who are confident that God is the Lord of the Church and of the world, priests familiar with liturgical and personal prayer. A confidence enabling them to draw others into the mystery of faith; priests with an energy for mission, seeking to hear where God's passion for the world is to be focused now.'

Carrying concerns

Such an attitude concerning the primacy of desire for God is also the antidote to the way we sometimes find our empathy results in an inability to let go of a pastoral concern. I know St Paul tells us to 'Bear one another's burdens, and in this way (...) fulfil the law of Christ' (Gal. 6.2) but we also need to remember Jesus' invitation: 'Come to me, all you that are weary and are carrying heavy burdens, and I will give you rest' (Matt. 11.28). It does parishioners no good if a priest becomes overburdened by their concerns. It may be difficult, but whatever we carry needs placing on Christ's altar, where it belongs, and if we can't let go, we need to see our spiritual director.

Although the college closed in 1973, the Community of the Resurrection (CR) at Mirfield continues to prepare men and women for ordination, and the Church has been enriched by their commitment to this formation. As one priest wrote: 'My time at Mirfield taught me the grammar of priestly ministry, primarily in silence and in sharing the rhythm of the monastic offices. I very much doubt I would have had the capacity to persevere in my ministry if I hadn't learned some of these deep structures.'

To the Glory of God

A fruitful pastorate springs from an interior life
of contemplation of and communion with God.
(Raynes CR, in Curtis CR 1977, p. 172)

Ordination can be a means of exercising profound ministries. But, as I explored in *Enfolded in Christ*, it's easy to lose touch with that foundational call into an ever-deepening, loving, relationship with God from which all else flows. Clergy need always to consider Jesus' thrice-repeated question 'do you love me?' (John 21.15f.); I remember how Br Bernard SSF was fond of saying: 'Get it right with God first, bruvvy', which helps keep a balance between the ministry's clergy exercise and the relationship into which they – like all – are called.

It is easy for other things to become the focus and maintaining a disciplined life can be hard. In 1845 Fr Benson SSJE wrote: 'If we are to be a Church, surely our clergy must become holy' (Letter to W. J. Butler, 16 December). He longed to see

> a body of men [sic] gathered together, whose life of what the world would call self-denial and poverty, should be cheered with the greater joy than the world can give, by the sympathy of kindred hearts and the spiritual strength of abundant means of grace. (Congreve SSJE and Longridge SSJE 1916, pp. 227–9)

In 1858 he gave a retreat for the newly formed priestly Society of the Holy Cross (SSC) and later said about clergy in London's East End: 'It is true that although they were living in all the rigours of the Religious Life, they were not living under vows, but they were wholly dedicated – at any rate their great leader [Fr Lowder of St Peter's, London Docks] was wholly dedicated to God … we must remember that vows do not constitute the Religious Life (which) is the life of the Spirit within the heart of those who take the vows. *The vows are the shelter of the Spirit*' (Hanbury-Tracy and Carter 1900, p. 166f.). Another example of this is the way Fr Wainright, Fr Lowder's successor, was described as 'to England what the Curé d'Ars is to France' (Menzies 1947, p. xvii – the Curé was St Jean-Marie Vianney, Patron of Parish Priests) not least because of his love for the poor and the way he spent an hour in prayer in church at the start of each day.

Dispersed communities

SSC survives (for men only), while various fully inclusive, dispersed priestly associations have emerged. The Society of Catholic Priests (SCP) and Sodality of Mary, Mother of Priests

(SMMS) exist for their sanctification, but neither require those vows associated with the Religious Life. The Oratory and Sisters of the Good Shepherd (O/SGS) comprises celibate members, ordained and lay, at the heart of whose life lie 'Seven Notes':

> The aim of the Oratory (and Sisters of the Good Shepherd) is the adoration of God in the service of our Lord Jesus Christ and the imitation of his most holy life. Its fellowship and discipline are intended to encourage and direct its members in achieving this aim. Their membership will remind them that they can carry out their vocation of worship and service only in communion with the Good Shepherd and in the power of the Holy Spirit. (*Introduction to the Seven Notes of the Oratory*)

The Company of Mission Priests (CMP), another celibate male community, was founded during the Second World War to serve evacuees in poor areas, eventually ministering in some of the vast council estates which sprang up to replace slum housing. Since the 1990s they have been profoundly re-formed through the spirituality of the Congregation of the Mission begun by St Francis de Sales. He believed that sanctity for anyone is best expressed as faithfulness to the will of God through what the present moment is asking of us. No matter what our feelings might be, we are to fulfil that will with loving thankfulness.

A holy priesthood

As the mission of the Church concerns the world's relationship with God her ministers need to take that relationship seriously and beware when accidie develops and what began as inspiring dulls through the years. If Morning Prayer becomes rushed before the 'real work' of the day begins, Evening Prayer optional and retreats seen as 'reading weeks' (as important as study is) we see indications that priorities might have become forgotten. In a similar way, it is possible for the 'mission' of the church to become so activist that the first commandment is obscured.

Placing worship first puts us in a right relationship with God and reminds us of the need for humility. Without humility the temptation to want status, show how clever or successful we are, seek 'promotion' and so on can begin to undermine a calling. The common habit means, among other things, that Religious priests aren't distinguishable by their dress, nor do their hoods display their academic achievements. If we are tempted by pride or envy, we need to pray for the opposite – the 'lowest place', as Fr Kelly SSM wrote in the *Principles* (VIII). Pride can blind us to the way such temptations are undermining: 'Do not think too much about yourself', Principle XXII tersely states, 'your own opinions and feelings may well be of less importance than they seem to you.'

Priests and leaders

My Franciscan years also taught me that priesthood and leadership are not the same. This is powerfully illustrated by the way a Religious community gathers around the altar for the Eucharistic prayer, affirming that we worship a God who is a community of Persons inviting us to share in their life. Br James Koester SSJE reminded me that Religious leadership emerges from its place in a circle, whether that be the priest presiding at the Eucharist or the community's Abbess/Guardian in relation to the community. The latter may be also a lay member, as was true until recently for all communities of women, emphasizing the servant nature of priesthood, for it is the *community* that is the focus rather than an individual.

Everyone needs to beware the lure of 'promotion'. If feelings of being overlooked arise, they need to remember that God sees the truth of who we are. Given attention, such feelings can easily grow, so we need to pray: 'Take from me this desire, Lord, and keep me humble. Let me be satisfied by doing small things well, according to your will.'

Of course, we can feel that few understand or really care about the pressures and problems we face: ministry can be very lonely. It's then the temptation to find distractions, which can become addictions, can be great. Remember, it's not how much we do, how successful we are, or what we achieve that matters; what matters is that our heart is being converted into the Heart of Christ. Look to him, for there lies true joy and peace.

Fools for Christ

Francis of Assisi had a high regard for clerics, but it is also important to have a healthy indifference to them. Priests can seem a caste apart, but the holiest are those who can laugh at themselves, for laughter, emerging from the joy of God, echoes heaven. Honest laughter serves humility: it deflates self-pride and can prevent us becoming too self-conscious about 'getting it right'. I remember how, in training altar servers, the Master of (Chapel) Ceremonies at Kelham would lie on the sanctuary floor to make sure their feet never lifted more than an inch off the ground so making them appear to glide, a practice some-one laughingly described as preparing them for 'high mass at Wellington barracks'.

Holy common-union

For all Religious the Eucharist is 'the centre around which their life revolves ... it is the heart of their prayer life' (SSF *Principles*, Day 15) in the same way the Passover is for Jews. It is the Divine Mystery of Christ's liberating sacrifice into which we are constantly drawn; the thankful offering of our lives to the Father, the common-union in which his brothers and sisters share. Here our Master is present as he was to his disciples, the focus of our praise, prayer and devotion.

The Eucharist reveals a deeper appreciation of what it means to be Church, the Body of Christ, where each member needs the other. Like Baptism, it's a sacrament to be lived as we allow the dynamic of Christ to be expressed through us as he – with love and trust – offers us and his life to the Father.

> The Eucharistic mystery, both offered and lived, is therefore the heart of our life. Through it our whole being is united to Christ's perfect offering, our work, our sin, our joys and sorrows, the unknown depths of ourselves, all is taken up, transfigured that it may become a means through which is continued the divine work of redemption. (CSC, *Rule*)

Here I sensed community at a deep level, a community that was challenging and which reflected the nature of the Church. It informed and shaped us but wasn't a gathering of perfect people. There is no ideal community; Christianity is about living through paradox. We weren't there because we necessarily 'liked' each other, but because Jesus told us to love one another and this is the sacrament of Love, a celebration having deeper appeal than simply being a (possibly) moving service. Here, Love reveals itself in Christ's real presence which can touch our innate goodness so that, through us, his love can engage with the world. In one of St Ambrose's hymns set for Morning Prayer we sing:

> And Christ for us for food shall be,
> From him our drink that welleth free,
> The Spirit's wine, that maketh whole,
> And, mocking not, exalts the soul.
> (*English Hymnal*, 52)

That sacrificial communion needs to penetrate the whole of (priestly) life. Every aspect of the Eucharist can reveal God's reign, which is what makes the lives of holy priests so powerful. This is seen especially through someone such as the Curé d'Ars, whose inspirational life was centred on the Eucharist and informed by membership of the Franciscan Third Order.

> I have learnt to know that it is very possible to go to Mass daily and not to go to Jesus at all interiorly, and to go to

confession weekly and never to repent ... [The Mass] is an everlasting Sacrifice, and if we are true to our Communions, we are always in the attitude of those who are assisting at the everlasting Sacrifice. (Burne 1948, p. 111)

Unlike some other forms of worship, the Eucharistis is focused on what *Christ* does, rather than what we do; for just as earthly matter becomes divine so we are to be changed into his Body. It is a mystery to be celebrated and lived as the heart is shaped by Christ's oblation 'of himself once offered'. His life informs ours, for an oblation is never a pleasant thing and can involve the apparent loss of what makes life meaningful.

Week by week and month by month, on a hundred thousand successive Sundays, faithfully, unfailingly, across all the parishes of Christendom, the pastors have done this just to make the *plebs sancta dei* – the holy common people of God. (Dix OSB 1964, p. 744)

It is an offering moulded by thanksgiving as we let go to let God work with us. God wants to refashion our demanding ego through the gentle Divine Will so that Will may be done on earth as it is in heaven. It is Christ's abandonment of himself to his Father, seen most graphically in the crucifixion, that enables his Body to be glorified.

I am so grateful to have been formed in contexts where the Eucharist is understood to be a joyful yet demanding mystery celebrating our transformation. The altar at which we stand is the earthly foundation stone on which the heavenly Jerusalem is revealed, where the Lamb is the true Priest and Victim (Rev. 5). That is the primary vision needing to be present to the priest's inward eye whenever they preside; that Divine Mystery that points to the hiddenness of God in everything. I'm grateful because it helped me understand we are to shift awareness from self to the Other, something which can be very helpful for those introverts who find they can become caught in inner confusion or when the eye is taken by the congregation.

In the body of Christ the Eucharist unites heaven and earth,
carrying the whole of humanity to the throne of God
in the offering of Christ to the Father.
We receive God in Christ,
our humanity re-made in the image of its maker.
(It) is the centre of our worship. (CHN, *Rule*)

Adoring the Host

As host and chalice are consecrated, I realize the value of
silently adoring him who looks kindly upon creation. It was
through that moment I came to understand how contemplative
living prevents us being driven into the exhausting way of the
activist. Such living flows beyond the Eucharist, for the Word
we contemplate and the Sacrifice that's offered are made real as
we seek to love God with all our hearts, enabling us to discern
'everyday holiness'.

> Just sit
> in the Real Presence.
> Christ is here –
> in that Tabernacle, Aumbry, Pyx –
> the flickering light of transcendent glory
> tells us.
> Always there
> saying, 'I am Love,
> so love one another.'
> Adore that sacred Presence.
> He is the One with us,
> His wounded Body enfolding ours,
> His sacred Blood
> flowing through the world's veins.
> Tell him you love Him and hear Him say –
> 'I love you too.'

Blessed, praised and hallowed
be the Bread of Life
who makes us drunk on rich Wine
flowing from His Sacred Heart.

We are to give attention to God in the whole of creation, something aided by spending time in the presence of Jesus in the Blessed Sacrament, gazing on him as he looks, lovingly, upon us. This approach to prayer has no other purpose than that the world, and we who pray, might be enfolded in God's transforming presence. For this reason, some communities value times of prayer before the Blessed Sacrament, which was a particular focus of the Community of Reparation to Jesus in the Blessed Sacrament (CRJBS: 1869–2006). This prayerful devotion can lead us from a sense of emptiness and loss to transformative encounter. Rather than running from feelings of desolation, filling our lives with distractions, it is here God connects with us within the well of the soul. Priests have a responsibility to enable people to realize they are called to be open to these depths of divine encounter. Each day we are called to offer ourselves to Christ as he abandons himself to the Father. Then, as Fr Kelly said, 'if you have given your whole life to God why should you prefer to lose it in this way rather than in that?' (SSM, *Principles*, XII).

Behold, each day he humbles Himself
as when he came from the royal throne into the
    Virgin's womb;
each day He himself comes down to us, appearing humbly;
each day He comes down from the bosom of the Father
upon the altar in the hands of the priest.
As he revealed himself to the holy apostles in true flesh,
so He reveals himself to us now in sacred bread.
(St Francis of Assisi, *Admonitions*, 1:16–19)

A Prophetic Life

Your vocation is none other than the call of God,
who wills you to live to the praise of his glory –
the light of that glory he has revealed
in the face of Jesus Christ.
God in his mercy has called us sinners
to witness to the fellowship of the mystery of Christ.
See your calling as a token of the calling of everyone.
Your function within the Church and to the world
is to be a sign.
(Franciscan Hermits of the Transfiguration, *Rule*)

The priestly vocation to be immersed in the things of God mirrors that of the Religious, and each has a prophetic character for they witness to the primacy of the Word. But Religious vows also identify important elements of that character. As the *Rule* above continues: 'First: to be a sign of Christ in his detachment from all to belong to all – a sign of Christ's poverty by which he made all men rich, a sign of Christ's chastity that he became the brother of all and the Father of the poor, a sign of Christ's obedience that he might give to everyone his true freedom.'

Justice, peace and the integrity of creation

Religious have always sensed a call to stand with the poor and many have been involved in movements for justice and reconciliation, often at great personal cost. Tragically, for example, the peacemaking efforts of members of the (Anglican) Melanesian Brotherhood in Guadalcanal during a period of civil unrest led, in 2003, to seven of them being martyred.

This call to work for the common good echoes around the world. In Godly obedience, it cries out against the sin of self-centredness which does such damage, while affirming aspects of the Divine Commonwealth, calling for liberation from whatever prevents that freedom affecting the whole of creation (Rom. 8.18f.). The world doesn't exist to satisfy our disordered desires or to make us happy at whatever cost. It exists, in union with us, to glorify its Creator. We won't 'find ourselves' through our freedom to use it in whatever way we want but through serving God and neighbour and living in thankful, harmonious union with creation.

Because God is in all things and all things reflect the splendour of their Maker, everything is to be reverenced. It is to our shame that we've raped the planet and gorged on creation's fruits: contemplating what we're doing, it is argued that the forces of technology are having a blinding effect, causing our disordered desires to have a controlling effect on some. Are we at the point of a major, catastrophic shift or can we repent and, as contemplatives know, reconnect with the living cosmos (Rom. 8.22f.)?

> Franciscans seek to worship and serve God in His creation and are therefore pledged to the service of others and to respect for all life. We aim at a simple lifestyle and at self-denial, living in solidarity with the poverty of the world and accepting its claim upon our stewardship. (https://tssf.org.uk/about-the-third-order/introduction-to-the-third-order/)

Francis, Patron Saint of the Ecological Movement, looked at creation with the eye of his heart and, in love with the Creator, realized a marvellous love for all things. His heart-wisdom revealed the interrelatedness of creation, leading him to address everything as 'brother' or 'sister'. And because 'There is no longer Jew or Greek, there is no longer slave or free, there is no longer male and female; for all of you are one in Christ Jesus' (Gal. 3.28) his followers have also sought to break down divisive barriers and welcome all.

> In beautiful things (Francis) saw Beauty itself; all things were to him good. 'He who made us is the best,' they cried out to him. Through his footprints impressed upon things he followed the Beloved everywhere; he made for himself from all things a ladder by which to come even to his throne. (Thomas of Celano, 'Second Life of St. Francis', in Habib, 1972, pp. 494–5)

All this can only be realized through the eye of the soul, helping us sense the wonder of our own being. I find myself experiencing that wonder beneath my feet, of those unseen, primal organisms communicating through underground microscopic fungal filaments, whenever I walk through magnificent woodlands. That 'wood-wide web' helps me understand that, together with all that exists, we are connected with the cosmos through a hidden network of prayer:

> Francis has made us see
> How music fills the skies;
> A glorious psalmody
> Which cannot fail to rise
> As God is praised by humankind,
> By water, sun, moon, stars and wind.
> (SSF *Hymnbook*, 37)

This (ancient) wisdom is reflected in that important collection of spiritual writings, the *philokalia* (Love of the beautiful/ good). In it there's reference to the way we come to 'the knowledge of the speech of all creatures' (French 1930, p. 45), a gift with which God can grace us along the contemplative way. Such cosmic intimacy requires us to treat creation with loving respect and care because all things bear the touch of their Maker. Our generation needs more contemplatives.

Like most communities, Hilfield Friary is one example of many who welcome guests wanting to share in their life: opposing all that denies our common humanity they have been developing ways of living in greater harmony with the land, creating conservation programmes reflecting the sacredness and beauty of Mother Earth:

> At the Friary we try to value the mundane, ordinary things of life, and find a balance between manual work, social engagement, rest and recreation. Everyone plays some part in the daily tasks of the Community – work in the garden or on the land, cleaning and maintaining the buildings, baking bread and preparing meals, sharing in the admin-

istration and offering hospitality to guests and visitors. All these things are related to the rhythm of daily prayer and worship in the Chapel, through which we are renewed in the life of Gospel, making for an integrated ecology which is spiritual, social and environmental. (https://hilfieldfriary. org.uk/spirituality/)

9

Life Together

The Witness of Life

This is my prayer,
that your love may overflow more and more
with knowledge and full insight
to help you to determine what is best,
so that on the day of Christ you may be pure and blameless,
having produced the harvest of righteousness
that comes through Jesus Christ
for the glory and praise of God.
(Philippians 1.9–11)

For almost 2,000 years, Religious Life has offered examples of that common life into which Christ calls us and which every church is to express. In joining the Franciscans I became part of a community that didn't depend on natural families, who Jesus rarely mentioned (except to indicate some needed to leave them: Luke 14.25–26). His disciples were to be part of a new creation.

Religious Life has developed important insights into community. Valuing the other, no matter how different, it offers sorely needed wisdom about how diverse peoples can live as one on our small, fragile planet.

Imagine that the world is a circle, that God is the centre, and that the radii are the different ways human beings live. When those who wish to come closer to God walk towards the centre of the circle, they come closer to one another at the same time as to God. The closer they come to God, the closer they come to one another. And the closer they come to one another, the closer they come to God. (Abba Dorotheus of Gaza, *Instructions* VI)

Everyone has a place

Today Sister Margaret presided at the Eucharist and Sister Valerie led the Intercessions. Nothing odd about that – except both needed the aid of walking frames; one was 90 and the other 94. It's refreshing to find places where the elderly aren't marginalized and everyone has a place reflecting the way that, in the Body of Christ, all belong.

The holy-wholeness experienced by many who visit communities comes, in part, from the common life in which all contribute to the creative yin-yang of prayer and service, study and recreation, solitude and community. 'We must learn,' said Fr Benson when addressing the 'special vocation' of sickness, 'that those do most who obey most truly. It is not those who have most energy, or learning, or wealth, or skill who do most for God; but those who give themselves up most truly to do His will' (Benson SSJE 2020, p. 52).

Religious Life witnesses to a way contrasting with our competitive culture where ability and success are promoted, profitability is its focus, sport seems more about winning than playing and even computer 'games' frequently encourage users to fight and destroy their opponents. What, I wonder, might this be doing to our individual and communal soul/psyche?

Yet, standing for different values, this Life is often sidelined or ignored. At best it encourages its members to build holy common-unity, and take seriously the place of the marginalized, weak and vulnerable. It is intended to reflect the 'new

Jerusalem', that fresh expression of our humanity which begins with the way each member seeks to love the other. 'They will love also with a special affection', say the *Principles of the Society of St Francis* (Day 27):

> ... those to whom they are united within the family of the community, praying for each individually and seeking to grow in love for each. They must be on their guard against all that injures this love: the bitter thought, the hasty retort, the angry gesture; and never fail to ask forgiveness of any against whom they have sinned. They must seek to love equally with others those with whom they have least natural affinity. For this love of one another is not simply the welling up of natural affection but a supernatural love which God gives them through their common union with Christ. As such it bears testimony to its divine origin.

Christ comes in every guise, encountering us when we are least prepared, often in unexpected, unchosen ways. How should I respond to the constant stream of those asking for help, for money, for a listening ear? I have turned from him many times, yet still he comes. What matters is that I don't allow my heart to harden, that I learn compunction with each encounter so that I'm moved towards greater compassion and openness.

Isn't that what every parish community needs to discover? It can be hard when our attention is on ourselves and our desires – blind to the other unless they're attractive to us. But still Christ comes.

Life together

One of the benefits of communal life is that it overcomes isolation. The Elders were drawn to share resources, spiritual and material, for their mutual benefit while finding safety in numbers. It was in community I recognized how much I needed to feel loved and that caused many problems, ultimately addressed through meditating on God's love, the compassion of my community, recognition that I was loved and the wisdom of a good spiritual director and therapist.

Another gift of shared life is that it provides the means of loving God through our neighbour 24/7 by overcoming any tendency to self-centredness as each learns from the other. Instead of hiding we need to be open so we can be known, for that is how we grow into wholeness. That was the problem for our 'primal parents': they experienced shame, hid themselves and found they were excluded from Paradise. But any community that contains people seeking to show loving hospitality offers another Eden.

Saved by my neighbour

Make me
a still place of light
a still place of love
of You
your light radiating
your love vibrating
your touch and your healing
far flung and near
to the myriads caught
in darkness, in sickness
in lostness, in fear

make a heart centre here
Light of the world.

Mother Osyth OSB, Malling Abbey

I don't mean to suggest that every community is filled with paragons of virtue – far from it – and many found/find me difficult. But, like annoying colleagues or family members, they can help the beauty of holiness/wholeness to emerge. For their presence invites us to practise disinterested love, nurture compassion aided by humility and exercise self-denial. To love them despite (because of) their 'faults' for they are also the beloved of God, offering a chance for us to work against our inclinations (logs and splinters: Matt. 7.1f.), helping us realize something of our 'shadow' side. They are God's gifts.

Those brothers I found most difficult revealed the measure of my love of God (1 John 4.20). Yet while such people can be the grit that enables the pearl, grit can, sometimes, be too painful to live with and there were times when, for communal well-being, a brother needed to move on.

I know that when I react strongly to another I need to stop and check what's happening. I might not agree with or disapprove of what someone's saying or represents – I might even see them as an 'enemy' – but they're offering a means for growing in mercy, compassion and reconciliation. Isn't the way we open our heart to this 'enemy' a way of redeeming the world's brokenness – of breaking the chains of hatred? Doesn't our welcome of those whom some cast aside offer a means of healing and wholeness even when it is, apparently, abused or rejected?

A Religious community is a microcosm of the world and the smaller the community the less anyone is able to hide, so rather than an escape it involves facing your 'self' as that self emerges through the eyes of others.

Catholic Christianity is for all, for the whole of man, and for all time. The Church cannot be national, nor exclusive, it is for all. It is only in the Church that real equality is to be found – where all are baptised with one baptism and all partake of one bread. (Raynes CR 1959, p. 57)

Hospitality

Sometimes, I wonder what heaven is like but know I've tasted it from time to time, mostly in the context of relationships – which can also be purgatorial (that's the way to heaven). Many don't realize that our faith declares that the God in whom we believe isn't a solitary father-figure dominating creation from the summit of existence, but a Trinity of unique 'Persons' living in hospitable unity where difference is celebrated in Oneness of Being:

> Now the Catholic Faith is this: that we worship one God in Trinity, and the Trinity in Unity;
> Neither confusing the Persons: nor dividing the substance. For there is one Person of the Father, another of the Son: another of the Holy Spirit;
> But the Godhead of the Father, and of the Son, and of the Holy Spirit is all one: the glory equal, the majesty co-eternal. (Athanasian Creed)

While 'seeing' God in Christ, this Trinity is beyond beings we can conceive. Yet Religious communities are meant to be sacraments of this divine life together where – within the charism of the community – difference and diversity, valued and celebrated, can enrich the whole. Whether living an enclosed life or finding the world your cloister, it reflects the diversity of humanity only to be fully realized in union with the Trinity.

The Trinity offers an understanding of that hospitable union sensed when encountering communities where many find a sense of sanctuary. In what can be experienced as a chaotic world, 'people – whether Christian or not – feel "safe" here', as one sister said about her convent. 'There's something about the regular rhythm of our life with Offices and Eucharist, times of meditation and meals open to guests that provides stability at a time when many feel a bit lost. Norms of behaviour are recognized; boundaries exist and there's an intentionality of living in the love of God for the sake of the kingdom. We offer places of living prayer. Every community – whether comprising three or thirty members – needs to reflect the hospitality of God who says: "you belong, welcome to the New Jerusalem!"'

All guests who present themselves are to be welcomed as Christ, for he himself will say: I was a stranger and you welcomed me. (RB 53.1)

Although not all Religious vow stability, the fact that some communities have occupied the same buildings for many years means that, while congregations change and people come and go, there's a profound sense of continuity about them. What does their witness of holy 'life together' say to businesses moving away leaving people jobless, or churches that lose a sense of being part of their neighbourhood? What might it say about the need to develop rhythms of prayer?

This splendour of holiness marks the Communion of Saints – but saints aren't easy to live with because they can challenge unredeemed aspects of life. We might be skilled at our profession, exemplary teachers, proficient in spiritual practices – but have we learned to put self aside so that Christ can live through us? How transparent are we to the gospel?

> To the single eye
>   comes the sight of God himself,
>   everywhere perceived.
> (Malling Abbey, *Haiku*)

Rule for holy living

Every community, like the Body of Christ, is made up of its varied members yet, while it is always greater than the sum of its parts (for Christ is invisibly present) its life depends on the (spiritual) health of all. Just as society functions best when each person fulfils their potential, and churches grow when congregations are united in the love of God, so a Religious community flourishes when members are animated by the primary call to seek God and God's will.

Religious Orders will have a Rule expressing their unique calling through the norms of their life by offering a balance of prayer, intimacy, study, work and rest. It will express how members can live together for the good of all.

A rule of life is basically an articulation, a breaking into the open light of consciousness, of values, practises, habits, and conceptions that would otherwise remain tacit, taken for granted ... Once identified, named, owned and celebrated their latent energy is released. (*Rule of the Society of St John the Evangelist*, p. 121)

While the Beatitudes might be described as the primary Rule for Christians, a personal 'Rule of Life' can help free us from self-centredness and remind us of the ways we are called to live out our faith and learn to integrate our wills with God's ('thy will be done').

In creating my own Rule I tried to recall that it needs to be informed by the law of love and daily conversion of life; it doesn't exist for itself but as a means whereby God's kingdom can be realized on earth. A rhythm of prayer needs to pulse through each day aided, for clergy and others, by the Office. Of course, it's not easy to set aside the time and, yes, it requires discipline, but through it the wonder of Christ's relationship with the Father in the Spirit becomes an increasing part of life. So, retreats are vital.

And because prayer needs to become part of life's natural rhythm it needs expressing during times of relaxation and we need to consider how that can be done. 'Sabbath' recognizes the place of Godly rest and while Sunday may be a working day for some, there still needs to be a day on which we can enjoy a certain freedom and not simply fill it with different things to do, while also allowing for the place of prayer – which needs to be the foundation of any Christian well-being programme.

Next, we need to consider the time given to deepening our intimacy with families/friends, together with reading, study and the means whereby we express the generosity of God. How can my lifestyle express the way of the Beatitudes? For it's the *whole* of life which is to be sanctified so God's Reign can be expressed. A Rule needs to help with that ongoing *conversatio morum* identified by Benedict, and the Society of St John the Evangelist offers a useful online guide to 'Growing a Rule of Life'.

Like Religious Life, a Rule needs to be concerned with the restoration of all things in Christ (Eph. 2.11f.). That's the

mega-picture which begins to be realized in mini-ways: there's
no point in protesting about how people don't care for the
planet if we're not growing in a sense of our own responsibility, or lamenting breakdowns in society while not seeking to
be peacemakers and reconcilers; no point in complaining that
people are less interested in religion if we aren't growing in our
relationship with God. Our calling is:

> ... not merely to witness to Christ
> but to respond to the Christ
> who lives in and among us
> and is present in all our encounters.
> We are to be points through which
> may be continued
> God's work of redemption
> and reconciliation.
> (CSC, *Rule*)

IO

The Hidden Monk

The Full Stature of Christ

Speaking the truth in love, we must grow up in every way
into him who is the head, into Christ,
from whom the whole body,
joined and knitted together by every ligament
with which it is equipped,
as each part is working properly,
promotes the body's growth in building itself up in love.
(Ephesians 4.15–16)

Those words, and Paul's following instructions about living
in Christ, resonate in the hearts of many. Recognizing that in
Christ we see both the image of God and what humankind
might be (Col. 1.15), Religious Life reveals ways we can be
moulded by him and how, in him, this matter of what being
human concerns becomes clear: he, the true image of God, the
new Adam, reveals humankind's perfection:

*Christ shows us
what we are restless to become.*

That's why it is said there's a 'hidden monk' (or nun) in each of
us, as explored in Greg Peters' *The Monkhood of All Believers*.
That doesn't mean we all need to join monasteries or convents;
rather our vocation concerns reflecting the Body of Christ
whose loving, joyful, humble, obedient, sacrificial life of prayer

and praise is to flow through ours to the glory of God and the well-being of creation. Our hidden monk/nun embodies wisdom concerning what becoming fully human involves by realizing how the divine enables that: this 'monastic' opens the doorway to heaven and one's true self. Whether single, partnered or living in community, we are called to this way of holiness, to be part of the communion of saints – and saints are those who have struggled to put self aside and be consecrated to Christ and his Reign.

> The purpose of the Religious is to be like the candle flickering next to the tabernacle. Their job is to simply be there, in front of the tabernacle, flickering away in prayer when no one else is able to be there. (A Carthusian)

Religious Life is a microcosm – the struggles faced by its members are often the same as those faced by everyone: how individuals do battle is usually hidden in their hearts. All life's hopes and joys, fears and conflicts can be found within any community. 'Religious Life,' said Fr George Herbert, co-founder of the Community of the Holy Name, 'is not a different life from Christian family life but … a *picked sample* of what the Christ-like life should be, a continual protest against selfishness, self-indulgence and self-will which are the world's temptations in every age and clime' (Dunstan 2005, p. 75). It challenges the Church to remember where true riches are to be found.

> What is it to be consecrated to Jesus Christ, if we are not absorbed in His love? (Benson SSJE 2020, p. 156)

Those pioneering Anglican Religious heard Jesus say: 'I came to bring fire to the earth, and how I wish it were already kindled!' (Luke 12.49) and were set ablaze by him. Are we? We may not be called to such a Life, but we are called to say 'yes' to Christ, to be 'leaven in the lump', transformative presences, 'signs not solutions' as someone said of the Community of the Transfiguration.

Individually, none can solve the world's needs, but we *are* called to the 'way of perfection' to help build up, in the words of Dom Gregory Dix OSB, the *'plebs sancta Dei* – the holy common people of God' (Dix OSB 1964, p. 744). Religious Life reminds us that Christianity doesn't simply concern personal sanctification but is for the sake of God's Reign.

> Let us give ourselves to God that he may accomplish his will, which is the participation of the creature in the loving action of the Creator.
> (Shaw 1969, p. 5)

Those who claim Religious are hiding from the 'world' are, in a way, right: it *is* a life hidden with Christ in God in a way that enables the individual to be formed by him. Some look to change the world, and many for forms of 'spirituality' but, from the Desert Elders to those nineteenth-century pioneers, Religious Life shows us that the heart of society *and* the human heart need to be changed. It isn't a Life centred on satisfying individual wants, although it can be deeply satisfying; it involves simplicity of life that all may live, self-giving love rather than self-fulfilment, and desire for others' good rather than our own.

Thankfully, there are still those who hear the call to give themselves in this way and step out in faith and trust. As one writes: 'This has never been an easy life, or an escape from life, and just as it is rooted in our baptismal vocation, so it is rooted in the paschal mystery, *behold, dying we live!*'

> Jesus, set me on fire
>   with your love.
> Stir my heart to see your glory
>   in all things
>   and sing your praises.
> Show me what you want me to do for you,
>   my King,
>   and your Kingdom.

One in Christ

It reminds us that boundaries of nation and state are, in the end, transitory when compared with the Reign of God. Religious may be scattered across the globe, but they witness to the truth that, in Christ, there is 'no longer Jew or Greek ... for all of you are one in Christ Jesus' (Gal. 3.28). Our Faith isn't compatible with nationalism or any notion of 'my country before all else'; it's a life that affirms faith's folly, a way that speaks into our deepest needs as individuals who must live – or perish – together.

It witnesses to the fact that the quest for what Christianity calls 'true riches' (Luke 16.11) is infinitely worthwhile. We need what it teaches – about compassion and sacrifice; contemplation and humility; commitment and faithfulness; community and solitude; repentance, prayer and praise. Where those pioneers travelled, we need to follow.

> Clarity of mind,
> Simplicity of spirit,
> Unity of heart.
> (Malling Abbey, *Whittled Words*)

The 'monkhood of all believers'

Some point to the universal appeal of monasticism, whatever its expression, and affirm that the monk/nun is the archetype of what it means to be human for s/he expresses a longing for unity with creation and Creator.

This was apparent in the lives of Sr Dora Pattison CHR (1832–1878) and Br Edward Bullstrode (1885–1953). Sr Dora was a member of the Community of the Holy Rood where she trained in the basics of nursing, enabling her to eventually undertake that heroic work in Walsall for which she is still celebrated as the 'Florence Nightingale of the Midlands'. Edward spent time with the Society of St John the Evangelist in Oxford and the essence of the Religious Life continued to inspire him as he went on to found the Village Evangelists. Like them, many sense a yearning greater than any longing for family, wealth, power or prestige, something which requires renouncing all that prevents attaining that goal of at-one-ness with the One beyond all while serving those in need.

There's a way we are all called to live the Religious Life, a way that involves being constantly centred into God (stability) as we seek to be changed into God's likeness (conversion of life), denying our ego-serving self through detachment from 'things' (poverty), focusing our deepest desire (chastity) and bending our heart to catch the voice of our Creator (obedience). Just as the scholar and athlete train themselves, to be in-Christ means honing our hearts so his life emerges through ours (1 Cor. 9.24f.). All we do either helps or hinders that: we work to live not live to work; eat to live, not live to eat; desire to love God in all things, not desire all things so we can be god-like.

It is not what we do, but how we do it that matters. It is not different work, but a different way of doing our work that God asks of us. The habit of doing common things with un-common care is what will make us saints.

(Mother Emily's Message, 5 June 1900, Community of the Sisters of the Church)

Dispersed Yet One

O that my ways were made so direct,
that I might keep your statutes!
I will meditate on your commandments ...
and give attention to your ways.
(Psalm 119.5, 15)

Whatever its expression, Religious Life is a response to the One who identified as 'I am who I am', or 'I am who I am becoming' (Ex. 3.14), requiring the abandonment of the self to that way which leads to what Jesus spoke of as 'eternal life' (Matt. 19.29).

> Our Community is a living cell of that Body. Therefore, we are to be a means through which Christ lives on earth in adoration of God our Creator, desiring that the divine glory may be manifest, God's sovereign rule come, and purposes of love be accomplished. And also we are to offer ourselves in love as Christ did for the world's healing and reconciliation with God. (CSC, *Rule – Our Religious Vocation*)

Apart from those called to the solitary way, many new expressions of Religious Life involve 'dispersed communities' whose individual members, in the tradition of the Elders, live apart while coming together for certain occasions. Being 'in the world' their daily lives are informed by one or other of the great traditions of Religious Life. Among them are:

• The Brotherhood of St Gregory (BSG) and the Order of Anglican Cistercians (OC/OCCO). Members might be single, married, partnered, ordained, or lay, working or retired. Similar communities, for both women and men, exist throughout the Anglican Communion witnessing to the fact that contemplation is at the heart of Christianity and isn't just something done if there's time when the 'real work' is over.

• The Community of the Holy Family (CHF) is another Order offering new life to the Church after, seemingly, 'dying' in 2010. A group of Episcopalian women (USA) believing in 'empowerment through education' have developed a dispersed Order whose Rule is based on that of the original CHF. It is composed of those who, like many early pioneers, are prepared to go and help change the lives of those whom society has 'written off'.

• Companions of Jesus of Nazareth are motivated by the witness of Blessed Charles of Jesus (Charles de Foucauld) whose devotion to the Sacred Heart of the Eucharist mirrored the way he saw Christ hidden in all people. An ecumenical Order, each Companion seeks to live their 'own Nazareth', the place in which God has planted them, sharing the life of their neighbour, after the example of Jesus to whom they abandon themselves.

• The Single Consecrated Life offers a way for those who, having 'smelt the aroma' of God, are drawn to its source and feel called to embrace celibate, eremitical (hermit) life. Many live in the 'desert' of our cities, finding support through belonging to a network of solitaries who embrace a life of chastity. Other communities, like the Anglican Order of Preachers, Worker Brothers and Sisters of the Holy Spirit, etc., are also signs that the Church is to be a contemplative community in the world – each member seeking to be like yeast as they nurture Christ in the heart, just as Mary held him in her womb for the world's sake.

Hidden 'monastics'

The life of a 'hidden monk/nun' isn't easy and cannot be simply an escape from that life of 'quiet desperation' the 'mass of men live' (Thoreau, *Walden*, chapter 1), nor a matter of preferring your own company. Rather, it's realizing the primacy of the first Commandment – to love the Lord your God with all your heart – and, finding a joy in that which permeates all else, becoming a witness to the Church (and society) of a vocation so easily forgotten.

Those called to this way usually arrive at a time when they begin to get listless and bored, a state the Elders defined as 'accidie' which can involve a sense of Divine absence. Yet this 'howling wilderness waste' (Deut. 32.10) masks an eternal Presence and in the rush of everyday life, when feelings (the 'passions') get the upper hand, hermits are reminders that your feelings aren't you; they cannot penetrate the soul. They might emerge from deep within and are often strong, depending on what's experienced, but we are not to be entrapped or controlled by them – especially the negative ones – nor give them an importance they don't have. For, as those Elders came to realize, that's exactly what Satan wants.

> The habit and tonsure by themselves are of small significance; it is the transformation of one's way of life and the complete mortification of the passions that makes a true religious. (Thomas à Kempis, *Imitation of Christ*, 1.17)

Rather than dwelling on the 'self', greater peace and strength comes by giving thanks for what is good and focusing on that in others, wondering at God's presence in creation, expressing compassion and saying:

> *(Breathe in)* Jesus Christ, Son of God ...
> *(breathe out)* have mercy on me, a sinner.

Third Order of St Francis

Over time there have been many expressions of dispersed Religious Life, one of the most lasting being that inaugurated by Francis of Assisi. After some men first gathered around him, followed by women led by St Clare, others appeared – married or single – wanting to adopt the charism of his life who weren't called to celibacy, and these he named the 'Order of Penitents', his 'Third Order' (today 'Secular Franciscans' in the Roman Catholic Church).

One of the first Anglican shoots appeared in India in the 1920s and the Order is now present throughout the Anglican Communion. Formed through a novitiate, members profess to live by Three Aims: to make Christ known, to spread love and harmony, and to 'live joyfully a life of simplicity and humble service after the example of Saint Francis' (*Form of Profession*, Third Order SSF). They seek to express that same commitment to non-violent compassionate living and the well-being of creation which marked the life of their Patron.

Associates, Companions and Oblates

It is also possible to express aspects of Religious Life through becoming an Associate, Companion or Oblate of an Order. Adopting a Rule reflecting its charism, members keep in touch in differing ways – Oblates of the Sisters of the Love of God, for example, declare their aim to be the glory of God by witnessing to Christ's 'repairing of human disobedience by the sanctification of their lives through their union with the life of the Incarnate Son of God'. They go on to declare they will 'endeavour by their discipline, prayer and constant self-oblation to share in all that still has to be undergone by Christ for the sake of his body the Church (Col. 1:24)' and use their oblature to lead them in the power of the Holy Spirit to union with God through Christ.

The beauty of holiness

Holiness is informed by the life of Christ. Religious Life reminds us that it doesn't come from church teachings, biblical injunctions, or historical liturgies, but from our relationship with Jesus. We are to express that relationship in the earthiness of life, homely service of neighbour, care for the whole of creation, and as in my case, loving attention to one's partner. Holiness is the child of the Beatitudes, the fruit of habit and grace, informed by a certain simplicity and detachment. Given to divine Love we're to have a heart listening for God's call in and through our relationship with Jesus.

> Jesus, it is you I long for ...
> you, I seek ...
> you in whom I long to abide ...
> you, the Word, must shape my life ...

Taking time to stop, notice and wonder, allowing all our bodily and spiritual senses to respond enabling us to become re-embodied, fully incarnate and conscious of ourselves as co-creators. Our relationship with nature is deepened by that sense of wonder expressed by the psalmist. Wonder at the mystery beneath outer forms teaches us humility and prevents us believing we are masters rather than simply sisters and brothers. Wonder (at God in all things) prevents utilitarianism, literalism and profitability from becoming our gods.

Nurturing the contemplative is for the sake of humanity lest we fall into the trap of knowing the price of everything but the value of little. Walk a little slower, stop and delight; to paraphrase an insight of Pierre Teilhard de Chardin (cf. *Hymn of the Universe*, 1969): become 'priests of creation' offering your Eucharist as you gaze on the world: 'make holy, Father, these gifts of creation by sending down your Spirit upon them like the dewfall, that they may become for us the body and blood of your Word.' Paradise, often emerging from extremely unpromising material, becomes tangible every time we open our eyes in wonder at the mystery before us and offer our sacrifice of thanks and praise.

> With manual work it is so easy to slip into the secular mentality of 'getting things done' and consequently resenting difficulties ... Again, there is needed an increased dependence upon the Holy Spirit to work faithfully in cooperation with the Providence of God, and to be thankful for the resources, material and human, which are available. (Gregory CSWG, *Community Report*, 1983)

Designed by St Charles of Jesus

What Do You Seek?

So, Lord, when that last morning breaks,
Looking to which we sigh and pray,
O may it to thy minstrels prove
The dawning of a better day.
(*English Hymnal*, 57)

The day I arrived at Hilfield to begin my new life I had to meet
with the Bursar. After briefly explaining some practicalities he
looked at me and suddenly said: 'Buried or cremated?' After a
moment to recollect myself I replied, 'What's the difference?'
'Burial's cheaper if you die here, the cemetery's at the bottom
of the Avenue and we do it ourselves.' And so 'we' did. Over
the years I've carried coffins down the Avenue and helped bury
many brothers, residents, wayfarers and others who had found
a home with us. Many's the time I've arrived at the grave holding, with three others, the coffin by its straps as we waited
to lower it and watched, with growing alarm, the clay sides
gently collapse (our cemetery was on a spring-line), praying
we wouldn't descend into the liquid mud with our departed
brother.

We are to live the folly of the cross which marks our whole life
and opens it to the power of Christ risen; 'always carrying in
the body the death of Jesus, so that the life of Jesus may also
be made visible in our bodies.' (2 Cor. 4.10f.) (CSC, *Rule*)

Death and dying

Community life brought me face to face with death's reality.
Increasingly I've noticed people talk of 'passing' and wonder
if a post-Christian society is more comfortable with that word
than 'death'. But for God's faithful people 'life is changed, not
taken away; and when our mortal flesh is laid aside, an everlasting dwelling place is made ready for us in heaven' (*Preface*,

Mass of the Dead). So, when we learned that a brother had died, we gathered to pray for them:

N, may Christ give you rest in the land of the living
and open for you the gates of paradise.

At Hilfield we washed the body and kept overnight vigil with the departed in the small chapel of St Mary of the Angels – an old, whitewashed coal shed attached to Juniper House next to the cemetery – before the funeral. For a while, my cell over-looked the cemetery where, each All Souls' Day (2 November), we would process to pray for all lying there. Death was an ever-present reality, one we might ignore but will all experience. So how we prepare for that moment when we pass to Judge-ment would seem to be of some importance.

One of the hymns we sang at Requiem Masses was the Rus-sian 'Contakion of the Dead':

Give rest, O Christ, to thy servant with thy saints:
where sorrow and pain are no more;
neither sighing but life everlasting.
(New English Hymnal, 526)

It is hauntingly beautiful and figures among my favourites because the words affirm that in returning to the earth our Creator will bring us to life with the saints. Naturally, we might be concerned about the loneliness that can occur as mortal life ends and, while we hope there won't be too much suffering, we can train the eye of our heart to gaze on God so that we look forward to being drawn more deeply into Love. That's another reason we need familiarity with solitude: it helps us realize our deepest desire for union as we give attention to that voice invit-ing us to be present to the Presence.

It's a yearning echoed by those first words of Jesus, accord-ing to St John's Gospel – 'What are you looking for?' (1.38) – a question which, if we let it pierce our hearts, will assist the voyage of faith. Asked of those beginning the monastic jour-ney it has, in whatever form, only one response: 'I seek the mercy of God and his will for me.' So begins a new life: searching, learning and discovering the meaning of mercy, a process which – hopefully – transforms the heart. A life which is about communion and participation – barred from an earthly garden we're invited into the heavenly City.

Often a crisis causes us to question ourselves at depth: what the 'world' offers – its lures and distractions, fading wealth and notions of success that don't satisfy – suddenly falls apart. That's what happened to me: more than once I've hit a wall or known I've messed up. Realizing the depths of sin into which we have sunk or glimpsing who we are can cause a shock, or we might discover that what we thought would make us happy hasn't, and we see the shallowness of our lives and hear, in a fresh way, that question: '*What do you seek?*'

Of course, our response can be very tentative. When Jesus asked it of two of John the Baptist's disciples (John 1.38f.) they didn't immediately respond with, 'the answer to life's big questions'. Nor did they ask for health, peace, happiness, or any of the other things we often say we want. Cautiously, they simply replied, 'Where are you staying?' to which Jesus responded, 'Come and see.' Thousands have done just that; stayed with a Religious community to see what difference their life in Christ makes (as ought to be true of every church), and when they encounter God at work it can resonate in the heart. The witness of a life where the emphasis isn't on me and what I can get but on the Other and how we might be changed, become more fully human, can speak powerfully.

The reign of God

Founders of Religious Orders recognized the dangers of wealth and chose to be poor with the poor Christ. They showed solidarity with them as Christ did at his incarnation – that 'preferential option for the poor' – ridding themselves of whatever prevented finding their treasure in him. In face of the division between rich and poor they chose the way of compassion, cooperation and common-wealth, realizing that the world's goods are for the equal benefit of all. This has been especially important for those who, like St Clare of Assisi, are called to the contemplative life – people who have recognized the challenge of the Mother of God in her radical Magnificat: 'He has filled the hungry with good things: and the rich he has sent empty away', words that can be rendered powerless by music intended to beautify, not confront.

Religious Life has proclaimed the riches to be found in Christ amid a world whose fundamental purpose has become the unsustainable accumulation of wealth, whether by individuals, families, or multinationals often ruled by demagogues. Corrupted human nature emphasizes 'me and mine', overlooks deceit and rejects Christ's gospel of the riches to be found through selfless simplicity. Not only does our possessive accumulation create the impression that the purpose of life is to gain as much as we can at the least possible cost irrespective of what it does to others or to the planet, it also needs defending. But to be a follower of Christ is to repent of such a misleading and dangerous manifesto and embrace and celebrate the way true riches can be found.

Pearl of great price

The heady days when thousands of Anglican Religious served the world and sang the praises of God may have passed, but we must never forget the witness of those courageous women and men who responded to Christ's call. Giving up the security of family they embarked on a way which, for centuries, none in that Communion had trod and, despite opposition, found joy in responding to the gospel imperative to follow Christ. They shared life with the most neglected and, in so doing, challenged the Church and society.

Without the witness of those consecrated to a life under vows expressing the essence of our faith, the Church might easily be absorbed by the world. Although it was less than 200 years ago that Anglican Religious Life was restored, it draws on the experience of 2,000 years, offering a treasury of wisdom without which we would be impoverished.

The place of Religious has been likened to that of Mary within the community at Pentecost, something that became apparent when I travelled around the Coptic Church and realized the important part monastic life plays for that (minority) Christian community. I'm quite aware not all live up to their calling; many struggle and some fall, but the calling continues to act as a beacon. For while churches in Egypt are important, it's the hidden lives of monastics and the ability to visit their communities (which people do in their thousands) that strengthens the life and witness of Copts at an existential level.

It becomes clear that the Reign of God is a reality in those communities and, in a land where the spiritual is still of fundamental importance, both Christians *and* Muslims (as I have seen) seek out those regarded as holy to help them on their journey.

The life of sanctification goes through the whole of time and covers the whole of space. It goes into the unity which is heavenly, the eternity which alone can be fully responsive to God ... Death is not an end: it is continuity, the gathering up of all we have done and are and will be. We take with us that which we have learnt in this life, for here and now God has given us Christ that we might live Christ. (Shaw 1969, p. 1)

We need to value those who consecrate themselves to God. '"How great an advantage it is to Christianity," wrote a friend of the contemplative way, "to have before the eyes of the world the example of them that wholly forgo it ... for the service of God, not the satisfaction of themselves"' (Allchin 1971, p. 3). They keep before us the realities of life in Christ revealed in the Beatitudes. In a society increasingly mindless of the divine and a Church often in danger from contemporary lures, Religious witness to the presence of God who calls us, showing that a life consecrated to saying 'yes' in prayer and service enables the revelation of that glory for which we were created.

Just over a century ago one of the great Cowley Fathers, Fr Congreve SSJE, wrote about the revival of Religious Life in words that are remarkably contemporary, challenging and prophetic:

The rediscovery of the consecrated life of self-sacrifice brings us a steady light of hope, in that it has no relation at all to any of the fantastic experiments which have flashed for a moment in our times ... We are no clever invention which is to put all to rights. We are no new experiment at all, we attempt nothing new. We represent only a resolve among a few serious Christians to go back as literally and fully as we can. The Religious (Life) expresses the conviction that Christ himself is the only power that is needed to save the world. ... The revival ... is not only a sincere attempt to apply the power of divine love and self-sacrifice directly and practically to the resolution of social discords in the world outside, but still more to bringing back the joy of her youth to the Church herself ... The Church had heavenly treasure to give but could only give them as far as she was well supplied with earthly means. But the awaking of the Religious Life meant the discovery that Christ's kingdom has powers of its own, independent of earthly support. (Congreve SSJE 1911, pp. 165–70)

Do his words ring in your heart? In the face of greed, possessiveness, and egoism we need to seek the blessing of Christ's holy Poverty. To combat a culture tempted by superficiality and sensuality we need to desire Chastity, that purity of the heart more concerned to show tender compassion than harsh condemnation. To fight self-centredness and pride we need to listen to the wisdom of Obedience. To tackle our addiction to noise and activity we need stability. And to purify the heart – ours and society's – we need to practise repentance which will change our lives for the benefit of the planet. This is the way of that conversion which lies at the heart of Christ's gospel, freeing us to love as he loved. We are never completely human unless we are in relationship with others: God did not stand apart but entered into the life and history of a people. Divine compassion opened its Heart and showed the way.

Love of the Holy One needs to be our focus and conversion of the heart our desire. Holiness is the ignored centre of human-being, as we respond to the mysterious Divine pulsing through all living things. To prevent the Church forgetting the Wisdom entrusted to it there will always need to be those consecrated to seeking to reveal this Mystery through their lives; to live as the Body of Christ for the sake of the world – to climb the heights or plumb the depths; to follow that long path which can be very ordinary but has moments of wonder – and pain. This is the Christian calling. What matters is that we keep going until, in the end, what we seek reveals itself.

Do not despair about yourself
for that has ruined many souls and vocations.
God who is infinite holiness has borne with you a long time;
you may well bear with yourself a little
until his grace shall have done its perfect work.
'*Beatus qui hic bene vixerit et feliciter consummaverit.*'
(Kelly SSM, *The Principles*)

Appendix 1

Some Traditional Religious Orders

Throughout the book reference is made to Religious Orders and listed below are those whose members assisted in writing, or are mentioned in, this book. There are many others. I'm very grateful to those who gave of their time and shared their wisdom, especially those who let me into the privacy of their Enclosures. The sense of dedication found among them was matched by humour and humility as we explored the treasures the Life has to offer the Church, as well as individuals. Information in this Appendix is mainly taken from the *Anglican Religious Life Yearbook* which lists Orders, both traditional and new. Information can also be found via individual websites.

Community of St Clare (OSC)
Founded at Freeland, Oxfordshire, in 1950 the community follows a contemplative tradition patterned on St Clare. It is the Second Order of the international Society of St Francis.

Community of St Mary (CSM)
Benedictine in ethos, 'the Sisters seek to live a traditional, contemplative expression of the monastic life, giving Evangelical witness to Jesus Christ as Lord and Saviour through Catholic faith and practice, empowered by the Holy Spirit in sanctified daily life'. The Eastern Province is comprised of two houses – in New York and Malawi – and the Southern Province is in Tennessee. They express their way of life through care for the body, the soul, and the earth. They seek to address the spiritual and temporal needs of society through a life of prayer and solitude, ministry to the poor, spiritual direction and hospitality.

Community of St Mary the Virgin (CSMV) – 'Wantage Sisters'

Called to respond in the spirit of Mary, Mother of Jesus, their life is centred in the worship of God through the Eucharist, Daily Office, personal prayer and reflection on the Scriptures. Founded in 1848 their ministries are various; they offer accommodation at Wantage and have a large body of Oblates and Associates.

Community of the Holy Family (CHF)

A dispersed group of women in the Episcopal Church USA restoring this Order founded in 1896 in the UK to educate and inspire young women. While being committed Episcopalians they are not affiliated with any diocese but 'live as hermits outside the Church' taking the charism of the Order with them into their various ministries.

Community of the Holy Name (CHN)

The sisters combine a life of prayer with service to others and being part of the communities in which they are called to live.

Community of the Resurrection (CR) – 'Mirfield Fathers'

Founded in 1892 this men's Order is 'called specially to public, prophetic witness to the Christian hope of the Kingdom'. In the UK it runs a Theological College, all sharing in the monastic round of prayer, worship and ministry.

Community of the Servants of the Will of God (CSWG)

This mixed community, founded by Fr Robert CSWG the year after William of Glasshampton died (1937), is rooted in the eremitical tradition of the contemplative life, uniting silence, work and prayer in a simple lifestyle based on the Benedictine rule. They are especially concerned with uniting the traditions of East and West and accordingly use the Jesus Prayer. There are also Associates who live in the spirit of the Community.

Community of the Sisters of the Church (CSC)

An international body of lay and ordained women whose patrons, St Michael and all Angels, point them to a life both of worship and active ministry, of mingled adoration and action. Their particular dedication is to the mystery of the Church and the Body of Christ in the world.

Community of the Transfiguration (later, Franciscan Hermits of the Transfiguration)

Founded in 1965 by three Anglicans at Roslin, south of Edinburgh, the life was deeply influenced by the charism of Charles de Foucauld (St Charles of Jesus) and the Little Brothers and Sisters of Jesus, emphasizing the way of poverty and hospitality. Primarily a community of hermits, they sought to be ecumenical, something enabled when, in 1981, Fr Roland Walls become a Roman Catholic.

Community of St John the Divine (CSJD)

Together with their Associates the sisters offer a network of love, prayer and service 'under the patronage of the Apostle of Love'. Within the ethos of healing, wholeness and reconciliation they exercise a ministry of hospitality for people to come for times of rest, retreat and renewal as well as responding to the needs of the poor and the marginalized.

Company of Mission Priests (CMP)

Founded in 1940, this dispersed community of celibate, male priests share the vision of St Vincent de Paul. They endeavour to strengthen and encourage each other by mutual prayer and fellowship.

Fraternities of Charles de Foucauld and Companions of Jesus of Nazareth

Information is available from the Association of the Spiritual Family of Charles de Foucauld (www.charlesdefoucauld.org) which includes the Lay Fraternities and Jesus Caritas Priests' Fraternities, etc. The internet-connected Companions are another ecumenical group (www.companionsofjesusofnazareth.com) comprising both women and men.

Oratory of the Good Shepherd (OGS) and Sisters of the Good Shepherd (SGS)

Founded in 1913 in Cambridge (UK), the Oratory comprises male priests in various countries and in 2007 they helped develop the Sisters of the Good Shepherd. Bound together by a common rule, and grouped in geographical 'colleges', they meet regularly for prayer and support. Consecration to their life has the twin purpose of fostering the individual's personal search for God in union with their brothers/sisters and as a sign of God's kingdom.

Order of Anglican Cistercians (OC)

An order of uncloistered and dispersed Anglicans, open to celibate single or married men who live within the jurisdiction of an Anglican diocese in Great Britain. Their way of life is determined according to their Rule and in substantial conformity with that mapped out in the Rule of Saint Benedict. They are part of the Benedictine family.

Order of Julian of Norwich (OJN)

Founded in 1985 as a contemplative, monastic community for spiritual renewal in the Episcopal Church USA, they now comprise a worldwide family of affiliates committed to prayer, intercession and conversion of life.

Order of the Holy Cross (OHC)

An international Benedictine community for men founded in 1884 by James Huntington to provide a specifically North American expression of monasticism. It offers retreat facilities and has communities in Canada and South Africa.

Order of the Holy Paraclete (OHP) – 'Whitby Sisters'

Initially an educational order, they have diversified their work to include hospitality, retreats and spiritual direction, inner city involvement, preaching and mission. The Mother House is in Whitby with other houses in the UK and a long-standing commitment to Africa. Central to their life are the Divine Office and Eucharist, with a strong emphasis on corporate activity.

Order of St Benedict (OSB)

There are many independent monasteries, details of which can be found via: http://archive.osb.org/intl/angl/angl1.html

Society of All Saints Sisters of the Poor (ASSP)

They have an active ministry upheld and enriched by prayer. They aim to be channels of God's love in whatever way the Holy Spirit leads them, helping those who are in need by reason of age, health or social circumstance.

Sisters of the Love of God (SLG)

A contemplative Order with a monastic tradition founded in 1906, they draw on Carmelite spirituality and their life involves solitude to aid prayer. Under Mother Mary Clare, Father Gilbert Shaw influenced their development. The community includes Oblate sisters and others, including Priest Associates. They are responsible for Fairacres Publications, an important range of booklets covering a variety of topics on the spiritual life, monastic wisdom, theological reflection, Christian poetry and living.

Society of the Precious Blood (SPB)

Founded in a Birmingham slum in 1905, the community gradually felt called to a more contemplative life and eventually moved to Burnham Abbey, Bucks. With a Rule based on that of St Augustine their particular work is worship, thanksgiving and intercession and the Eucharist is central to their life, as is the watch before the Blessed Sacrament. They have Oblates and Companions.

Society of St Francis (SSF, CSF, TSSF, OSC)

The principal Anglican Franciscan order created by the uniting of smaller Orders in 1934. It comprises the traditional First Order for men and women (SSF and CSF), Second Order of Poor Clares (OSC) and Third Order (TSSF) of men and women – single or partnered – living 'in the world'. The 'Three Notes' of their life are humility, love and joy lived through an appropriate commitment to poverty, chastity and obedience. First

Order brothers and sisters share a common life of prayer, community and a commitment to issues of justice, peace and the integrity of creation. They are available for retreat work, preaching, counselling and sharing in the task of mission.

Society of St John the Evangelist (SSJE) – 'Cowley Fathers'

The oldest Anglican order for men is rooted in monastic traditions of prayer and community life and is critically engaged with contemporary culture. It was founded in Oxford in 1866 and, while it no longer exists as a community in the UK, there is a thriving North American congregation. Known for its retreat leaders, mission preachers and confessors, many of its members helped in pastorally caring for other Orders, primarily of women, and were involved in the formation of various communities.

Society of the Sacred Cross (SSC)

Part of the (Anglican) Church in Wales, they live a monastic, contemplative life of prayer based on silence, solitude and learning to live together. Taking vows of poverty, chastity and obedience their rule is Cistercian in spirit. They are dedicated to the crucified and risen Lord as the focus of their life and the source of the power to live it.

Society of the Sacred Mission (SSM) – 'Kelham Fathers'

Founded for the training of priests, the Society is now nurturing a community in Durham, UK as a new expression of the Religious Life. In addition, it continues to provide a centre for training in Spiritual Direction, a retreat house and location for quiet days and is working on suitable projects to make appropriate use of the historic assets to further Fr Kelly's vision.

Society of the Sisters of Bethany (SSB)

Following the Rule of St Augustine in the form modified by St Francis de Sales and St Jane Frances de Chantel, the Sisters seek, through their prayer and work, to reconcile the divided Churches. By simplicity of lifestyle they try to identify with those for whom they pray, sharing in Christ's work of intercession in the power of his Holy Spirit, under the patronage of Mary, Martha and Lazarus.

Single Consecrated Life (SCL)

A network of single, widowed or divorced mature Christians (men or women) committed to a life of prayer who have undertaken a period of discernment before making a temporary vow which can lead to a life vow.

Further information can be found online: http://anglicansonline.org/resources/orders.html

Information about 'new monastic communities' can be found via: www.societyoftheholytrinity.co.uk/.

Appendix 2

Commemoration Dates of Some Founders and Foundresses

January

10 Dorothy Louise Swayne TSSF (1887–1971);
    Lay founder, Third Order of the Society of St Francis
14 Richard Meux Benson SSJE (1824–1915)
19 Millicent Mary SPB (1869–1956)
23 Charles Gore CR (1853–1932)
29 Harriet CSMV (1811–1892); First Mother

February

9   Hannah Grier Coome SSJD (1837–1921)
12 Margaret OHP (1886–1961)
25 Rosina Mary and Helen Elizabeth CSF (Foundation Day)
27 Etheldreda SSB (1824–1913)

March

7   Joseph Crookston OSF (d. 1979)
26 Harriet Monsell CSJB (1811–1883)
28 William of Glasshampton (1862–1937)
31 Andrew SDC (1889–1946)

April

7   Roland Walls (1918–2011)
29 Teresa Newcomen CHR (1818–1887)

June

5   Emily Ayckbowm CSC (1836–1900)
6   Marion Hughes (1817–1912); first professed Religious in the Church of England since the Reformation

July

11   Benedict of Nursia (c. 480–c. 547)

August

10   Agnes Mason CHF (1849–1941)
11   Clare of Assisi (1194–1253)
18   Gilbert Shaw, William of Glasshampton and Robert Gofton-Salmond; co-founders of the Community of the Servants of the Will of God

September

7   Douglas Downes (1878–1957), co-founder SSF
23   Harriet Brownlow Byron ASSP (1818–1887)

October

4   Francis of Assisi (c. 1182–1226)

November

20   Priscilla Lydia Sellon SHT (1821–1876);
    Restorer of Religious Life in the Church of England
23   Algy Robertson, co-founder SSF (1894–1955)
25   James O. S. Huntington OHC (1854–1935)

Appendix 3

Prayer for Religious Life

Since 1992, the Church of England has recognized the Fourth Sunday after Easter as a 'Day of Prayer for Vocations to the Religious Life'. In 1997, the Roman Catholic Church instituted a 'World Day of Prayer for Consecrated Life' on the Feast of the Presentation of the Lord (2 February – usually transferred to the following Sunday).

For Vocations to the Religious Life

Ask and it will be given to you, search and you will find, knock and the door will be opened for you (*alleluia*)

V. Where your treasure is
R. *There your heart will be also (alleluia)*

Lord Jesus Christ,
in your great love you draw all people to yourself,
and in your wisdom, you call us to your service.
We pray at this time that you will kindle in the hearts
    of men and women
the desire to follow you in the Religious Life.
Give to those whom you call, grace to accept their vocation,
and thankfully to make the whole-hearted surrender
which you ask of them;
and for love of you, to persevere to the end.
This we ask in your name. Amen.

For all Religious

God our Creator,
you call men and women
to consecrate themselves to you
through a Vowed Life.
As we give thanks for their witness,
their prayer and their works,
so we ask you to enrich them in their poverty,
direct them in their chastity and
enlighten them in their obedience,
that through their life and worship
they may glorify you,
now and forever. Amen.

Bibliography

Francis of Assisi: Early Documents, Vol.1, New City Press, 1999
Hymns for Prayer and Praise, Canterbury Press, 2011
The Daily Office SSF, 1992
The Rule of the Society of Saint John the Evangelist, Cowley Publications, 1997
A Foundation Member OHP, *Fulfilled in Joy*, Hodder and Stoughton, 1964
Adams, Ian, *Cave Refectory Road*, Canterbury Press, 2010
Alexander, Georgina, *Following the Silence: a Contemplative Journey*, Gracewing, 2009
Allchin, A. M., *The Silent Rebellion*, SCM, 1958
Andrew SDC, *Meditations for Every Day*, Mowbray, 1934
Anson, Peter, *The Call of the Cloister*, SPCK, 1955
Atwell, Robert, *Celebrating the Saints*, Canterbury Press, 2016
Beer, M., *A History of British Socialism, Vol II*, George Allen and Unwin, 1919
Benson SSJE, Richard Meux, *Christian Progress;* George Congreve, 1911
―――― *Instructions in the Religious Life*, SSJE, 1927
―――― *The Followers of the Lamb*, London: Longmans, Green and Co., 1900
―――― *The Religious Vocation*, Wipf and Stock, 2020
Best, G. F. A., *Ideas and Institutions of Victorian Britain*, Barnes and Noble, 1967
Bouyer, Louis, *Introduction to Spirituality*, DLT, 1961
Burne, Kathleen E. (ed.), *The Life and Letters of Father Andrew SDC*, Mowbray, 1948
Carter, Richard, *The City is my Monastery*, Canterbury Press, 2019
Climacus, John, *The Ladder of Divine Ascent*, Paulist Press, 1982
Colin CSWG, *Listening, Silence and Humility*, CSWG, 2017
Congreve SSJE, G. and Longridge SSJE, W. H, *Letters of Richard Meux Benson*, Mowbray, 1916
Congreve SSJE, G, *Christian Progress, with Other Papers and Addresses*, Longmans, Green, 1911

Community of the Resurrection, *Mirfield Essays in Christian Belief,* Wipf and Stock, 2012

Curtis CR, Geoffrey, *William of Glasshampton,* SPCK, 1977

de Chardin, Pierre Teilhard, *Hymn of the Universe,* Fount, 1969

de Waal, Esther; *Seeking God – The Way of St Benedict,* Collins, 1984

Denis SSF, *Father Algy,* Hodder and Stoughton, 1964

Dix OSB, Dom Gregory, *The Shape of the Liturgy,* Dacre Press, Adam and Charles Black, 1964

Dunstan, Peta (ed.), *What's in a Name? A History of the Community of the Holy Name,* CHN, 2015

Felicity Mary SPB, *Mother Millicent,* Webberley Ltd, 1968

Ferguson, Ron, *Mole Under the Fence; Conversations with Roland Walls,* St Andrew Press, 2006

Francis SSF, *Brother Douglas,* Mowbray, 1959

French, R. M. (trans.), *The Way of a Pilgrim,* Philip Allan, 1930

Friendship, John-Francis, *The Mystery of Faith: Exploring Christian belief,* Canterbury Press, 2019

Frost ObOSB, R., *Life with St Benedict,* BRF, 2019

Gregory CSWG, *Monastic Life: Witness to the Spiritual Life of the Church,* CSWG Press, 2008

────── *Community Report 1983*

Habib, Marion (ed.), *Saint Francis of Assisi: Omnibus of Sources,* Franciscan Press, 1972

Hacking, R. D., *Such a Long Journey – a biography of Gilbert Shaw,* Mowbray, 1988

Hanbury-Tracy, A. F. S., and Carter, T. T., *Faith and Progress, the Witness of the English Church during the last fifty years, being sermons preached at the Jubilee of the Consecration of St. Barnabas, Pimlico,* Longman, Green and Co., 1900

Helen Julian CSF, *Franciscan Footprints: Following Christ in the ways of Francis and Clare,* BRF, 2020

Hilton, Walter, *Mixed Life,* Fairacres Publications, 2001

Howell, Arthur, *A Franciscan Way of Life: Brother Ramon's quest for holiness,* BRF, 2018

Jane SLG, *The Hidden Joy,* SLG Press, 1994

Janet CSMV, *Mother Maribel of Wantage,* SPCK, 1972

Jeanne and others SSC, *Continuous Miracle: A History of the Society of the Sacred Cross,* 2014

Kavanaugh, K. and Rodriguez, O., *The Collected Works of St. John of the Cross,* ICS Publications, 1991

Keller, David G. R., *Oasis of Wisdom,* Liturgical Press, Collegeville, 2005

Kelly SSM, Herbert, *An Idea in the Working,* SSM, 1908 (rep.1967)

Kirkpatrick, Bill, *The Creativity of Listening,* DLT, 2005

Longridge SSJE, W. H. (ed.); *Spiritual Letters of Father Congreve SSJE*, Mowbray,1928

Losada, Isabel, *New Habits,* Hodder and Stoughton, 1999

McEntee, Rory and Bucko, Adam, *The New Monasticism,* Orbis, 2015

Manton, Jo, *Sister Dora,* Quartet Books, 1977

Mary Clare SLG, *Encountering the Depths,* Fairacres Publications, 1993

Mary Stella SCP, *She Won't Say NO – the History of the Society of the Sacred Passion,* (undated)

Mayhew, Peter; *All Saints: birth and growth of a community,* 1987

Menzies, Lucy, *Father Wainright, A Record,* Longmans, Green, 1947

Merton, Thomas, *Praying the Psalms,* The Liturgical Press, 1956

Michael SSF, *For the Time Being,* Gracewing, 1993

Miller, John, *A Simple Life: Roland Walls and the Community of the Transfiguration,* St Andrew Press, 2014

Mumm, Susan, *Stolen Daughters, Virgin Mothers,* Leicester University Press, 1999

O'Brien SSJE, William B; *A Cowley Father's Letters: Selected from the Letters of W. B. O'Brien,* DLT, 1962

Packard, Kenneth G. *Brother Edward,* Geoffrey Bles, 1955

Palmer, Bernard, *Men of Habit: The Franciscan ideal in action,* Canterbury Press, 1994

Peters, G., *The Monkhood of all Believers: The Monastic Foundation of Christian Spirituality,* Baker Academic, 2018

Platten, Stephen (ed); *Oneness: The Dynamics of Monasticism,* SCM Press, 2017

Quinlan, William (Bill Lash CPSS), *The Temple of God's Wounds,* SPCK, 1953

Ramon SSF, *A Hidden Fire,* Marshall Pickering, 1989

———— *Franciscan Spirituality,* SPCK, 1994

———— *Heaven on Earth: Personal Retreat Programme,* Harper Collins, 1991

Raynes CR, Raymond, *Thoughts of a Religious,* The Faith Press, 1959

Rodriguez, O. and Kavanaugh, K. (eds), *The Collected Works of St John of the Cross,* SVS Press, 1994

Samuel SSF (ed) et al., *My God, My All, A Friar's Journey,* Society of St Francis, 2008

Samuel SSF, Nicholas Alan SSF and Simon Cocksedge, *Seeing Differently: Franciscans and Creation,* Canterbury Press, 2021

Seaver, George and Jennings, Coleman, *Tales of Brother Douglas,* A. R. Mowbray, 1960

Schiller CHN, Verena, *A Simplified Life,* Canterbury Press, 2010

Shaw, Gilbert, *The Life of Prayer,* 1959 (unpublished paper)

———— *A Pilgrim's Book of Prayers,* Fairacres Publications, 2000

———— *The Increase of Prayer,* CSWG, 2018

Sisters of the Church, The; *A Valiant Victorian,* Mowbray, 1964

Smith SSJE, Martin (ed.), *Benson of Cowley,* OUP, 1980

Society of St John the Evangelist, *The Rule,* Cowley Publications., 1997

Sophrony, Archimandrite, *St Silouan the Athonite,* SVS Press, 1999

Stebbing CR, Nicolas and Edwards OSB, Philippa, *Making Space for God,* Mirfield Publications, 2019

Stebbing CR, Nicolas, *Anglican Religious Life: A well-kept secret?* Dominican Publications, 2003

Underhill, Evelyn, *The Mystery of Sacrifice,* Morehouse Publications, 1991

Ward SLG, Benedicta and Russell, Norman, *The Lives of the Desert Fathers,* Cistercian Studies, 1979

Whitwell SGS, Sr Anita; *On Holy Ground,* Canterbury Press, 2008

Williams CR, Harry, *Becoming What I am,* DLT, 1977

—— *Poverty, Chastity and Obedience: the true virtues,* Littlehampton Book Services, 1975

—— *The True Wilderness,* Morehouse, 1994

Williams, Rowan, *The Way of St. Benedict,* Bloomsbury Continuum, 2020

Williams, T. J., *Priscilla Lydia Sellon,* SPCK, 1950

Wright, Robert, *The Evolution of God: The origins of our beliefs,* Little, Brown Book Group, 2010

Pamphlets and Papers

Cowley Evangelist, 1919

Haiku, Malling Abbey, 2003

Koinonia, The Common Life, Malling Abbey, 1998

Our Present Duty, Concluding Address, Anglo-Catholic Congress, 1923

The Principles of the First Order, Society of St Francis (private publication)

The Prophetic View of Monastic Life, CSWG, 1983

The Way Supplement, 64 (Spring 1989)

Whittled Words, Malling Abbey, 2003

Allchin, A. M., *The Theology of the Religious Life; An Anglican Approach,* Fairacres Publications, 1970

Allchin, A. M. (ed.), *Solitude and Communion,* Fairacres Publications, 2014

Colin CSWG, *Three Retreat Addresses and Talks,* Community of the Servants of the Will of God, 2017

Gregory CSWG, *The Prophetic View of Monastic Life,* Community of the Servants of the Will of God, 1983

Mary Clare SLG, *Aloneness not Loneliness,* Fairacres Publications, 2010

BIBLIOGRAPHY

———— *Silence and Prayer*, Fairacres Publications, 1972
———— *The Simplicity of Prayer*, Fairacres Publications, 2018
Shaw, Gilbert, *The Christian Solitary*, Fairacres Publications, 1979
———— *Prayer and the Life of Reconciliation*, Fairacres Publications, 1969
Ward SLG, Sr Benedicta, *Bede and the Psalter*, Fairacres Publications, 2002
———— *The Monastic Hours of Prayer*, Fairacres Publications, 2016
Ware, Kallistos, *The Power of the Name, The Jesus Prayer in Orthodox Spirituality*, Fairacres Publications, 1986

Unpublished Papers

Shaw, Gilbert, *Prayer: extracts from the teaching of Fr Gilbert Shaw*, 1973
———— *Recovery*, 1961
———— *Spiritual Warfare*, 1966
———— *The Life of Prayer*, 1959

Websites

Anglican Religious Life Yearbook, arlyb.org.uk
Society of St Francis, franciscans.org.uk/
———— (Hilfield Friary), hilfieldfriary.org.uk/
———— (Third Order), tssf.org.uk
Society of St John the Evangelist, ssje.org

Acknowledgement of Sources

Scripture quotations are from the New Revised Standard Version of the Bible, Anglicized Edition, Copyright © 1989, 1995 by the Division of Christian Education of the National Council of the Churches of Christ in the USA. Used by permission. All rights reserved.

The Custodian of the Standard BCP of the Episcopal Church in the USA generously allowed use of *The Psalms* on which no copyright was claimed. These were adjusted to comply with British orthography and usage and inclusivized in reference to human beings by the Society of St Francis who granted permission for use here.

Excerpts from the *Rule of Benedict* were taken from *A Reader's Version of the Rule of Saint Benedict in Inclusive Language*, edited and adapted by Sister Marilyn Schauble OSB and Barbara Wojciak. Text copyrighted © 1989 by Benedictine Sisters of Erie, Inc. All rights reserved. Adapted from RB 80 copyrighted © 1981 by the Order of St Benedict, Inc., Collegeville, MN. Used with permission.

Permission was kindly given by the following: Darton, Longman and Todd for a quotation from *The Creativity of Listening*; Dominican Publications (www.dominicanpublications. com) for extracts from *Anglican Religious Life*; Wipf and Stock for a quotation from *The Monastic Way*; the Sodality of Mary, Mother of Priests for an extract from their *Rule*; Mike Brown for his mother's pen-sketch of Malling Abbey; Regis J. Armstrong OFM (ed.), for excerpts from *Francis of Assisi:*

Early Documents: Volume I, New City Press, 2001 and SVS Press for a quote from *Saint Silouan the Athonite*.

Permission was also given by various Orders to reproduce material (if any copyright has been unwittingly transgressed or necessary gratitude not expressed, the publishers apologize and will rectify any such oversight in future editions):

Benedictine Sisters of Malling for various poems; the Community of St Mary the Virgin for extracts from *The Stations of the Cross* by Mother Maribel CSMV, from their *Rule*, and poems as quoted; Hilfield Friary and the Single Consecrated Life for quotations from their websites; the Sisters of the Love of God for extracts from the writings of Fr Gilbert Shaw, Sr Benedicta Ward SLG, Sr Stephanie-Louise SLG and their *Rule*; the Society of St John the Evangelist for quotations from *Benson of Cowley*, their website and *Rule*; the Community of the Holy Name, Community of the Servants of the Will of God, Community of the Sisters of the Church, Sisters of the Good Shepherd, Franciscan Hermits of the Transfiguration, Society of the All Saints Sisters of the Poor, Society of the Sacred Mission, Society of the Sisters of Bethany for extracts from their publications; the Ministers General of the Society and Community of Saint Francis for quotations from the *Principles* of the First and Third Orders.